THE
ABCs
OF
Gold
Investing

How to Protect and Build Your Wealth with Gold

THIRD EDITION

Michael J. Kosares

Addicus Books
Omaha, Nebraska

An Addicus Nonfiction Book

ISBN 978-1-936374-83-0
This book is made available with the understanding that it has been prepared for informational purposes only and the Publisher and Author are not engaged in rendering legal, accounting, financial, investment, or other professional services. The information in this book is not intended to create, and the reading of it does not constitute a lawyer-client relationship, accountant-client relationship, investment advisor-client relationship, or any other type of relationship. If legal, financial, or investment advice or other expert assistance is required, the services of a competent professional person should be sought. The Publisher and Author disclaims all warranties and any personal liability, loss, or risk incurred as a consequence of the use and application, either directly or indirectly, of any information presented herein.

Library of Congress Cataloging-in-Publication Data

Kosares, Michael J., 1948-
  The ABCs of gold investing : how to protect and build your wealth with gold / Michael J. Kosares. — 3rd ed.
      p. cm. — (An Addicus nonfiction book)
  Includes bibliographical references and index.
  ISBN 978-1-936374-83-0 (alk. paper)
  1.   Gold--Purchasing--United States. 2. Investments—United States. I. Title.

  HG295.U6K67 2012
  332.63--dc22

                                              2012023270

Addicus Books, Inc.
P.O. Box 45327
Omaha, Nebraska 68145
www.AddicusBooks.com

Printed in the United States of America
10 9 8 7 6 5 4 3 2 1

Contents

To the true believers whose staunch advocacy laid the foundation for the contemporary gold market

Acknowledgments

The following organizations played an instrumental role in bringing this book to fruition: Gold Fields Mineral Services, Ltd. of London, England; the World Gold Council of New York; the St. Louis Federal Reserve Bank; the Gold Institute; the United States Mint; the Austrian Mint; the Royal Canadian Mint; the Gold Corporation of Australia; the South African Chamber of Mines; the American Numismatic Association; and the Mexican Consulate in Denver, Colorado, U.S.

For their prompt and complete support, I owe these organizations a huge debt of gratitude. Last but not least, I would like to thank Dr. Henry Swenson, who gave me the idea for this book in the first place. Without them, *The ABCs of Gold Investing* would have remained an unrealized dream.

Introduction

This book is a distillation of nearly forty years' experience working with private investors interested in adding gold to their investment portfolios. For many years, investors looking for a "how-to" guide on private gold ownership have gone home from the bookstore empty handed. With the publication of this guideline, a basic who, what, when, where, why, and how of private gold ownership is now available.

At the outset, I would like to make it clear that the purpose of this book is not to offer a proposed solution to the current economic problem now gripping the United States, Europe, and other nations around the globe. Insofar as it examines these problems, my intent is to explain their connection to the growing demand for gold in coin and bullion form. At the same time, anyone who reads the financial section of the morning newspaper and does not come away with a sense of unease should question whether or not he or she is processing the information correctly. A sense of anxiety, it would seem to me, comprises the rational response. Though we live in an age of gold, given its nearly ten-year bull market, it has not been in any sense a golden age.

It is to allay this sense of anxiety that so many, over the past decade and particularly over the past five years, have opted to diversify their portfolios with gold. Investment demand has reached a record level, as has demand from financial institutions, like hedge and pension funds, and lately from central banks. In the process, the gold price has steadily advanced on world markets to record highs. Over the past decade, the primary motivations for gold ownership have been asset preservation and wealth building as stock markets around the world went into a tailspin, yields trended toward zero, and confidence in the long-term purchasing of the dollar began to erode.

Now a new motivation for gold ownership has entered the market, one rooted in a dynamic shift in gold's supply-demand fundamentals. There is a sense of change in what is required in the modern investment portfolio to counter economic uncertainties over the long term. Gold, as the ultimate architect and protector of wealth, has recaptured its place as a permanent fixture in the asset portfolio, both public and private. This important change in sentiment strongly suggests the possibility of steady to increasing demand in the years to come as more and more investors come to view gold as a permanent, or semipermanent, portfolio fixture and a long-term savings alternative.

For many, this book could not have come at a better time. You now have in your hands a practical and comprehensive "how-to" manual for making an informed decision about gold ownership. Perhaps gold can offer you what it has offered countless others over the centuries: solid, unassailable protection against the gathering storm.

Michael J. Kosares
Denver, Colorado
2012

Indeed, there can be no other criterion, no other standard, than gold. Yes, gold, which never changes, which can be shaped into ingots, bars, coins, which has no nationality and which is eternally and universally accepted as the unalterable fiduciary value par excellence.
—Charles DeGaulle

Chapter 1

A is for . . .

Asset Preservation:
Why Americans Need Gold

*The possession of gold has ruined fewer men
than the lack of it.*
—Thomas Bailey Aldrich

The incident is one of the most memorable of my career. Never before or since has the value of gold in preserving assets been made so abundantly clear to me. It was the mid-1970s. The United States was finally extricating itself from the conflict in South Vietnam. Thousands of South Vietnamese had fled their embattled homeland rather than face the vengeance of the rapidly advancing Communist forces.

A couple from South Vietnam who had been part of that exodus sat across from me in my Denver office. They had come to sell their gold. In broken English, the man told me the story of how he and his wife had escaped the fall of Saigon and certain reprisal by North Vietnamese troops. They got out with nothing more than a few personal belongings and the small cache of gold he now spread before me on my desk. His eyes widened as he explained why they were lucky to have survived those last fearful days of the South Vietnamese Republic. They had scrambled onto a fishing boat and had sailed into the South China Sea, where the U.S. Navy rescued them. These were Vietnamese "boat people," survivors of the final chapter in the tragedy of Indochina. Now they were about to redeem their life savings in gold so that they could start a new business in the United States.

Vietnamese Kim Thanh gold bullion "bars" or leaves. In the mid-'70s, I purchased this type of gold from a couple who had escaped from Vietnam when Saigon fell. They fled with only a few possessions and their gold. For years, I kept the gold as a reminder of the power and importance of gold.

Their gold wrapped in rice paper was a type called Kim Thanh. These are the commonly traded units in Hong Kong and throughout the Far East. Kim Thanh weigh about 1.2 troy ounces, or a tael, as it is called in the Orient. They look like thick gold leaf rectangles 3 to 4 inches long, 1½ to 2 inches wide, and a few millimeters deep. Kim Thanh are embossed with Oriental characters describing weight and purity. As a gesture to the Occident, they are stamped in the center with the words OR PUR, "pure gold."

It wasn't much gold—about 30 ounces—but it might as well have been a ton. The couple considered themselves very fortunate to have escaped with this small hoard of gold. They thanked me profusely for buying it. As we talked about Vietnam and their future in the United States, I couldn't help but become caught up in their enthusiasm for the future. These resilient, hardworking, thrifty people now had a new lease on life. When they left my office that day, there was little doubt in my mind that they would be successful in their new life. It was rewarding to know that gold could do this for them. It was satisfying to know that I had helped them in this small way.

I kept those golden Kim Thanh for many years. They became something of a symbol for me—a reminder of the power and importance of gold. Today, when economic and financial problems have begun to signal deeper, more fundamental concerns for the United States, I still remember that Vietnamese couple and how important gold can be to a family's future. Had the couple escaped with South Vietnamese paper money instead of gold, I could have done nothing for them. There was no exchange rate for the South Vietnamese currency because there was no longer a South Vietnam! Wisely, they had converted their savings to gold long before the helicopters lifted U.S. diplomats off the roof of the American Embassy in 1975.

Over the years, I have come to understand and appreciate the many important uses of gold—artistic, cultural, economic, and industrial. Gold is unsurpassed for jewelry and as a high-tech conductor of electricity. Gold has medical applications in dentistry and in treating diseases from arthritis to cancer. Gold plating is used in computers and in many other information-age technologies. In nanotechnology, it is used in a variety of cutting-edge medical diagnostic devices. As for its engineering uses, gold can be found in automobile anti-pollution devices, in jet engines, in architectural glass, and in a number of space applications. All of these pale, though, when compared to gold's ancient function as money, as an asset of last resort and an unequaled store of value.

The Stressed U.S. Economy

Some would have us believe that the financial crisis that began in 2007 with the residential real estate crash has been resolved, but nothing could be further from the truth. This crisis did not appear out of nowhere, descend upon the economy like a swarm of locusts, only to be addressed and sent on its way by a team of enlightened Washington policy-makers, never to be heard from again. It is, in fact, the latest manifestation of an ongoing crisis that has been with us for a very long time—one in fact that began in 1971 when the United States severed the link between the dollar and gold.

The multitrillion dollar bailout of the financial system that followed the collapse of Wall Street giant Lehman Brothers has already become the stuff of financial markets' lore, but it is not in any way a culmination, or an end, to the deeply rooted problems at its heart. At the time, Warren Buffet, the sage of Omaha, offered a warning: "[E]normous dosages of monetary medicine continue to be administered," he said, "and, before long, we will need to deal with their side effects. For now, most of those effects are invisible and could indeed remain latent for a long time. Still, their threat may be as ominous as that posed by the financial crisis itself." Those side effects amount to what is likely to be the next stage of the very same crisis "the monetary medicine" was intended to cure. What's past, as Shakespeare says, is prologue—a conclusion addressed in detail further on in this book in a chapter that deals with the Great American Bailout of 2008–2009.

At each new turn, we find that the *core problem* has not gone away, it has only deepened, become more widespread, and imposed itself on a wider swath of the American, and indeed, global public. Paul Volcker, the former Federal Reserve chairman and economic advisor to the Barack Obama administration, summed up the problem this way: "[U]nder the placid surface there are disturbing trends: huge imbalances, disequilibria, risks—call them what you will. Altogether the circumstances seem to me as dangerous and intractable as any I can remember, and I can remember quite a lot. What really concerns me is that there seems to be so little willingness or capacity to do much about it... We are skating on thin ice."

4

Far from disappearing, the disturbing trends Volcker mentions are at the heart of what's wrong with the international monetary system, and the primary driving force behind recurring problems in the financial sector. Many hope this deteriorating situation will simply disappear; but as Volcker indicates, in the absence of fundamental reforms, the situation will only worsen. Another former Fed chairman, Alan Greenspan, put it succinctly: "These trends cannot extend to infinity." In other words, in the absence of a genuine remedy, sooner or later there will come a final, and some think potentially calamitous, settling of accounts.

The disturbing trends affecting your investment portfolio:

- In 1970, the budget deficit was a meager $2.8 billion. By September 2011, it had reached $1.3 trillion—464 times the 1970 figure. Over the 40 years covered in the study, the annual addition to the national debt has risen by 8219%.

- In 1970, the accumulated federal debt was $436 billion. By December 2011, it surpassed the $15 trillion mark—up 3896% since 1971. This figure does not include so-called off-budget items like long-term Social Security and Medicare obligations, which balloon that figure by multiples.

- Exports and imports were roughly balanced in 1970. The last time the United States ran a trade surplus was 1975. By 2011 year's end, the trade deficit was estimated to be a dismal $470 billion for the year.

- In the process, the United States has gone from being the greatest *creditor* nation on earth to being the world's greatest *debtor* nation. In 1970, U.S. debt held by foreigners was a mere $12.4 million. By the end of 2011, it approached a dizzying $4.7 trillion, and was cited in a 2012 Gallup Poll of

Americans as a greater concern than the political situation in Iran, trade relations with China, or the financial situation in Europe. The problem of foreign-held debt has become so acute that some experts wonder whether the United States will be capable of pursuing its own monetary policy in the future, or whether the dollar is now hostage to our foreign creditors.

• Belying political claims that inflation is under control, the actual consumer price index has shot up nearly 500% since 1970, according to government-sanctioned measurements. Private economists say the number could be substantially higher.

• In 1970, the federal government collected a total of $196 billion in corporate and individual income taxes while it spent $195 billion. In 2010 it collected $2.34 trillion in taxes and spent $3.7 trillion. In other words, the real addition to the national debt that year was $1.36 trillion—a record. Thirty-seven cents of every dollar spent was borrowed.

The numbers in Figure 1 speak for themselves and do not require a great deal of embellishment. Over the years, the cumulative effect of these disturbing trends has been to steadily undermine the purchasing power of the dollar and leave in their wake a continuous stream of financial and economic crises of which the 2008–2009 breakdown is only the latest. Since 1971 when the United States severed the tie between gold and the dollar, the greenback has lost 82% of its purchasing power. The 1971 dollar, in other words, is worth 18 cents. Put another way, what the consumer could purchase for a dollar in 1971 now costs $5.54; and still another way, if you earned $50,000 in 1971, you would have needed to earn $277,000 in 2011 just to keep pace with inflation.

Figure 1 - Disturbing Trends 1970–2011

Item	1970	2011	% Change
Fed Expenditures (annual, billions)	198.6	3700	1,7630
Fed Interest Paid (annual, billions)	16.2	470	2,801.2
Accumulated Federal Debt (billions)	380.9	15223	3,898.6
Addition to National Debt (annual, billions)	14.4	1198	8,219.4
Fed Debt Held by Foreigners (annual, billions)	12.4	4660	37,480.6
Trade Deficit (annual, billions)	0.0	470	
Derivatives, notional (from 12/2000, billions)	95,199	707,569	643.
Consumer Price Index	37.8	226.7	499.7
Money Supply (MZM, billions)	469	10,619	2,164.2
Purchasing Power of Dollar	$1	17.5¢	-82.5
Dow Jones Industrial Average	809	12,218	1,409.9
Gold/troy ounce	35	1531	4,274.3
Dow Jones Industrial Average (2011)	11,670	12,218	4.7
Gold (2011)	1388	1531	10.3
Population (millions)	205	312	52.2
Median Income (annual)	9867	51,914	426.1

Notes: Annual Median income is for 2010. Federal Expenditures, interest on debt are projected for 2012 fiscal year. Federal Debt Held by Foreigners is for 9/31/11. Derivatives, notional from 12/2000. Statistics supplied by U.S. Census Bureau, White House Economic Statistics, Congressional Budget Office, U.S. Treasury Department, St. Louis Federal Reserve Bank, Bank for International Settlements, London Bullion Marketing Association. All figures in dollars except Consumer Price Index, Dow Industrial Average and Population.

Figure 2. **Purchasing Power U.S. Dollar, 1913–2001**

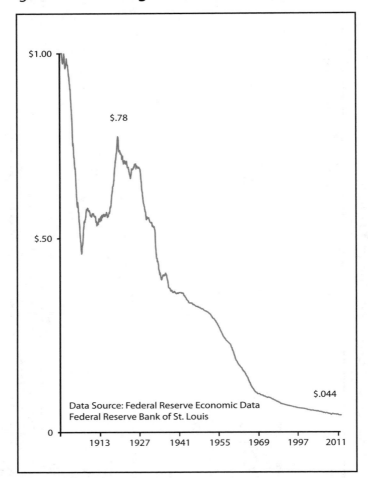

The 1980 dollar, over a period when Americans were constantly reminded that inflation was "under control," is now worth about 38 cents. Against two of the dollar's most tenacious competitors, the Swiss franc and the Japanese yen, its performance has been dismal. In 1985, it cost Americans 40 cents to purchase a Swiss franc and 0.4 cents to purchase a Japanese yen. In 2011, it cost $1.40 to buy that same Swiss franc and 1.3 cents to purchase a Japanese yen. In other words, the dollar has lost about 70% of its value against two of the world's major currencies over the past twenty-seven years.

Dollar debasement has become as American as baseball and the Big Mac—a fact of life which each of us lives with on a daily basis. Keep in mind, too, that the data used to build the chart in Figure 2 are based on the Bureau of Labor Statistics' (BLS)—a measuring stick the reliability of which has come under question in recent years. Shadow Government Statistics, for example, gauges the consumer inflation rate at a little under twice the BLS rate *using the same criteria the government utilized in 1990*, and nearly three times the BLS rate using 1980 methodology.

Needless to say, the long-term decline of the dollar represents probably the most troubling of our disturbing trends because currency depreciation can be technically infinite, or proceed until a final breakdown occurs. For a currency to fulfill its function as money, it must be accepted in daily transactions as a medium of exchange; it must be reliable as a store of value; and it must be generally accepted as a unit of account. In two of those functions, the dollar fulfills its role—as medium of exchange and as a unit of account. It is in the remaining function—as a store of value—that many, in both the private and public sectors, have begun to question its viability.

The Dollar Viewed from Overseas

Former Federal Reserve chairman Alan Greenspan once tellingly told Congress:

> "The imbalance in the federal budgetary situation, unless addressed soon, will pose serious longer-term fiscal difficulties. Our demographics—especially the retirement of the baby-boom generation beginning in just a few years—mean that the ratio of workers to retirees will fall substantially.

Without corrective action, this development will put substantial pressure on our ability in coming years to provide even minimal government services while maintaining entitlement benefits at their current level, without debilitating increases in tax rates. The longer we wait before addressing these imbalances, the more wrenching the fiscal adjustment ultimately will be... [G]iven the already-substantial accumulation of dollar-denominated debt, foreign investors, both private and official, may become less willing to absorb ever-growing claims on U.S. residents. Taking steps to increase our national saving through fiscal action to lower federal budget deficits would help diminish the risks that a further reduction in the rate of purchase of dollar assets by foreign investors could severely crimp the business investment that is crucial for our long-term growth."

Faced with the prospect of a diminishing market for U.S. debt overseas, the Federal Reserve might exercise the other option. It could very well crank up the printing press and flood the economy with money. In the aftermath of the 2008–2009 financial crisis, a good many economists believe that we have already made a turn down that road under the Federal Reserve chairmanship of Ben Bernanke.

Many of the world's central banks, particularly among emerging countries, have begun hedging their dollar reserves in the event of a full-blown currency crisis. As a group, central banks have become net buyers of gold in recent years after decades of being net sellers—a strong signal that the disturbing trends at work in the United States have begun to affect the way nation-states handle their dollar reserves. In 2011, central banks led by Russia, South Korea, Thailand, Mexico, and Turkey purchased 430 tonnes of gold—five times 2010s purchases and the largest volume of purchases in decades. In China, now the world's largest gold producer, the federal government purchased most of its domestic production in an attempt to shore up its dollar-based reserves. Simultaneously, it should be mentioned, China held steady on its acquisitions of U.S. Treasury debt. Though not a net seller of U.S. debt at this juncture, China is not a buyer either.

We have to assume that it is in the best interest of all nations, including China, to let the U.S. dollar down gradually, because it remains the world's principal reserve currency. Most nation-states have employed a gradual-ist approach. However, that could change as the U.S. federal government debt and fiscal problems worsen. In fact, People's Bank of China governor Zhou Xiaochuan warned the United States in 2011 that his central bank would continue diversifying its reserves in the absence of "responsible measures" with respect to the U.S. national debt. When China does make a foray into the gold market, its operations are kept totally secret. In 2010, however, it made a rare revelation that it had quietly accumulated over 450 tonnes of gold over the previous six-year period. True to its reputation for patience and steady, long-term progress toward its goals, China had taken the golden path and now they wanted the world to know about it. Other nation-states, as mentioned above, were quick to follow suit.

The United States is on a razor's edge with respect to its fiscal and monetary policies. As the world's primary reserve currency, the dollar is required to act as a reliable store of value if it intends to maintain that status, yet successive American governments have failed to fully address the issues undermining its value. Beyond the international repercussions, a recent *Washington Post* poll found 73% of Americans now doubt Washington's ability to fix America's economic problems. "The spreading lack of confidence," said the *Post*, "is matched by an upsurge in dissatisfaction with the country's political system and a widespread sense that S&P's (Standard and Poor's) characterization of U.S. policy-making as increasingly 'less stable, less effective and less predictable' is a fair one." That assessment from Standard and Poor's accompanied its August 2011 downgrade of the U.S. credit rating.

In a certain sense, Americans have begun to take the matter into their own hands. Politically, the general discontent among Americans has manifested itself in the electoral successes of the Tea Party movement on the right, and the Occupy Wall Street movement on the left. Financially, that public concern has manifested itself in booming demand for gold coins and bullion—a phenomenon that transcends both the political spectrum and national borders. The ever-present danger, beyond the steady erosion of the currency's purchasing power, is that these trends spin out of control, igniting a full-blown monetary crisis—an event that would threaten the value of all dollar-denominated assets including stocks, bonds, and personal savings. In such a context, asset preservation becomes the key issue, and gold, as you will see in the following section, becomes a means to an end.

Gold and the 1994 Mexican Peso Devaluation: A Lesson in Asset Preservation

An example of how gold protects wealth during a currency crisis can be seen in the December 1994 collapse of the Mexican peso. The now-infamous Christmas Surprise began with an announcement that the government had devalued the peso. Investor reaction was immediate. As soon as the devaluation was announced, long lines formed at the banks and sell orders piled up at brokerage firms, as alarmed investors attempted to get their money out of these institutions before they collapsed. A financial panic lurched into motion. Many were frozen out of the equity markets because they had dropped so precipitously. The peso was in a constant state of deterioration.

The inflation rate went to 50% immediately and stubbornly stayed at that level. Interest rates soared to 70%. Those with credit cards and other interest-sensitive debt teetered on the brink of bankruptcy simply because

Figure 3. **U.S Dollar/Mexican Peso Exchange Rate, 1994–1996**

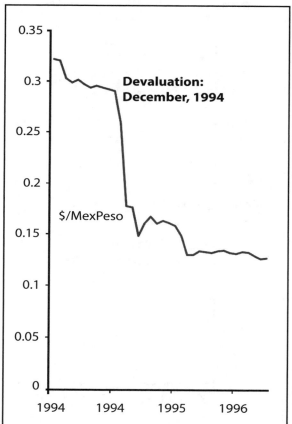

they couldn't make the interest payments. In the first year following the devaluation, the price of the peso went from 28.5 cents to 14 cents U.S. (Figure 3.) Over the ensuing years the peso continued to deteriorate and now trades in the 7-cent range.

The gold price, on the other hand, went immediately from roughly 1200 pesos per ounce to 2500 pesos per ounce—a mirror image of the peso's fall. Over the course of 1995, gold exceeded 3000 pesos—2.5 times its starting

Figure 4. **Gold Price in Mexican Pesos, 1994–1996**

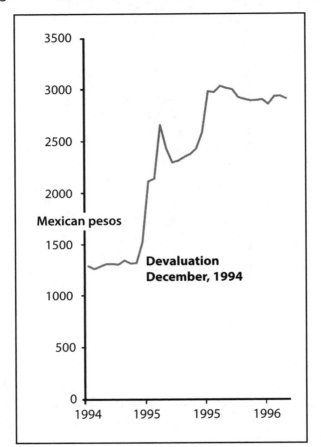

point, living up to its reputation as the ultimate disaster hedge (Figure 4).

Prior to the devaluation announcement, no warning was given the citizenry by the Mexican government or any of the country's major financial institutions. Unfortunately, no financial preparation on the part of the average citizen was possible unless one had the wisdom to diversify into gold, or a currency besides the peso, as a matter of course well before the crisis occurred.

Why Americans Need Gold

Although the United States, under the current fiat dollar monetary regime, would not suffer formal dollar devaluation, it is not immune to the ill effects of a sudden, full-blown financial panic. Gold, under such circumstances, would almost certainly behave like it did in Mexico during the peso crisis. In the wake of Lehman Brothers' collapse in 2008, for example, gold demand rose abruptly (see Figure 6—"U.S. Gold Eagle Sales by Year" in the following chapter.), and the price, after a brief, sharp correction, advanced over the next several months to new all-time highs.

Gold is traditionally viewed by people all over the world as the ultimate money, the historically tested and proven method for preserving wealth in even the most trying circumstances. It saved the French during their disastrous currency inflation of the 1790s. And it saved Americans during both the Continental Dollar collapse after the Revolutionary War and the Greenback inflation after the Civil War. The twentieth century was no exception. Gold was a bulwark during Nightmare German Inflation in the 1920s, the many hyper-inflationary blow-offs in South and Central America, the fall of Saigon, and the collapse of the Soviet Union in the early 1990s, as well as the multifaceted Asian Contagion in 1997, the currency debacle and bank panic in Argentina in 2002, and the 2008–2009 disinflationary meltdown in the United States and Europe. These are only a few of the more memorable occasions when gold played a critical role in asset preservation. Many more instances have ended up on the back burner of history.

It is a testament to gold that we have come to this juncture in the evolution of humanity—particularly in the United States, with all our modern contrivances—and still believe in its transcendence. According to a recent Gallup Poll (see Figure 5) Americans view gold as the best long-term investment over real estate, stocks, bonds, and savings accounts. "Gold," says Gallup, "is Americans' top pick as the best long-term investment regardless of gender, age, income, or party ID, but men, seniors, middle-income Americans, and Republicans are more enamored with it than are other Americans." Among those earning $75,000 or more per year, 31% chose gold as the best long-term investment, 23% real estate, 26% stocks, 8% savings, and 8% bonds. Demonstrating gold's wide appeal, 39% of Republicans polled chose gold as the best long-term investment, among Independents 33%, and among Democrats 32%. Overall, 34% chose gold, 19% real estate, 17% stocks and mutual funds, 14% savings, and 10% bonds.

"That one in three Americans see gold as the best long-term investment," concludes Gallup, "may indicate a bubble in the value of this precious metal—something that may be corroborated if gold continues to plunge as it did in (August, 2011). At the same time, this sentiment among many Americans may be related to the growing lack of confidence in the U.S. economy. This is particularly the case among upper-income Americans, who are now more pessimistic about the direction of the economy than their middle- and lower-income counterparts. The last time this happened was during the financial crisis of late 2008 and early 2009."

Gold today continues to play a critical and central role in the financial planning of both the world's central banks and countless private investors. The shared reasoning is simple and practical. Gold affords humanity precisely what it needs from time to time—the protection of wealth against the most threatening circumstances. Perhaps something in our ancestral subconscious places this value on gold. Perhaps it is something in our intellectual grasp of history. Whatever the case, gold has always been in the deepest sense a symbol of wealth, freedom, and enduring value.

Gold, it is often said, is the only asset that is not simultaneously someone else's liability. This is a very

Figure 5 - **Gallup Poll: America's Ratings of Best Long-Term Investment**

GALLUP POLL - Americans' Ratings of the Best Long-Term Investment
Which of the following do you think is the best long-term investment?

%	Gold	Real Estate	Stocks/ Mutual Funds	Savings Accounts/CDs	Bonds
Overall	34%	19	17	14	10
Men	41	16	19	10	9
Women	28	22	15	19	11
18–29	26	22	14	18	16
30–49	35	17	19	17	6
50–64	35	23	17	9	9
65+	41	13	17	11	12
$75,000	31	23	26	8	8
$30,000 to $75,000	40	18	16	13	8
Less than $30,000	34	17	5	23	14
Republicans	39	16	24	9	8
Independents	33	18	13	18	10
Democrats	32	21	16	13	12

*Reprinted with permission of Gallup Poll, Inc. *
Dennis Jacobs, Chief Economist

important concept to grasp. Once you understand it, little else is needed to justify the inclusion of gold in your investment portfolio. When you own a bond, a certificate of deposit, money market account, or annuity, you have essentially loaned an individual or an institution your money. To garner a return on that money, you are relying upon someone or something's performance. As compensation for that risk, you are paid interest on your money. Of course, stock values, as we so tellingly have come to realize over the last several years, rely on individual and institutional performance as well. If something goes wrong, the investor is at risk of losing all or part of the investment.

Gold, on the other hand, does not pay interest. As such, it does not rely on individual or institutional performance for value. If it did, gold owners would be at risk of default. Those who criticize gold because it fails to offer a return do not really understand gold's position as the fixed North Star of asset value around which all other asset values rotate. It is a stand-alone asset and the portfolio's centerpiece. In the ultimate sense, this is what money is and what money should be. It can always be relied upon when saved or held as a reserve asset in case of an emergency.

In *The New World of Gold*, analyst Timothy Green summed it up this way:

> "What John Maynard Keynes called 'the barbarous relic' still clings tenaciously to men's hearts. It remains the only universally accepted medium of exchange, the ultimate currency by which one nation, whether capitalist or communist, settles its debts with another... The importance governments still attach to gold as an essential bastion of a nation's wealth is more than equaled by ordinary people the world over, who see gold as the sheet anchor against devaluations or the hazards of war... Even the U.S. government, despite the

many anti-gold pronouncements over recent years, has issued its paratroopers and agents with 'escape and evasion' kits in gold. The Atlantic kit includes a gold sovereign, two half sovereigns, a Swiss 20-franc coin, and three gold rings; the Southeast Asia kit contains a gold chain, a gold pendant, two gold coins, and a gold wristwatch. 'The gold is for barter purposes, a Pentagon official explains. Actually, a London bullion dealer put it best: Gold is bedrock.' "

A is for Asset Preservation—Save gold, the ultimate store of value in times of economic uncertainty.

Chapter 2

B is for . . .

Bullion Coins: Portable, Liquid, and a Reliable Measure of Value

Do not hold as gold all that shines as gold.
—Alain de Lille

Gold for investment purposes is manufactured in two forms: coin and bar. Most of the gold owned by private investors around the world, however, is in the form of coins because of their portability and liquidity; that is, they can be converted to currency with ease. A third reason why coins are the preferred vehicle for gold ownership is that the minted coin is a standardized measure of weight and purity that current and future owners can rely on for value.

One of the first questions most prospective investors ask is, "What should I buy?" A good starting point is gold bullion coins like the U.S. Eagle, the American Buffalo, the Austrian Philharmonic, the South African Krugerrand, and the Canadian Maple Leaf. Bullion-related historic gold coins are another popular choice in that they go up and down with the gold price, but provide a unique additional advantage as discussed in chapter 8, "H is for—Historic Gold Coins." In contrast, jewelry, artistic objects, or very rare gold collectible coins should not be used for basic asset preservation because their gold value makes up such a small part of their overall value.

Figure 6. **U.S. Gold Eagle Sales by Year**

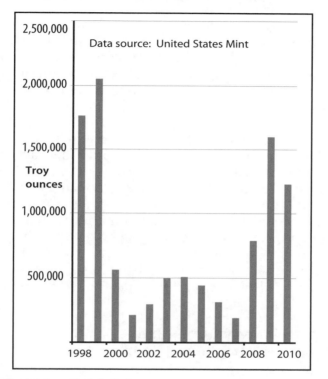

Most Popular Gold Coins

Many first-time investors believe gold is purchased in the form of the bullion bars depicted in the movies, but in the real world most investors buy one-ounce bullion coins. The end of this chapter includes a photographic catalog (Figure 7) of the most popularly traded gold bullion coins with their weights, purity, and face values. These coins track the gold price up and down, are dated with their year of manufacture, trade at marginal premiums over their gold melt value, and are very difficult to counterfeit. In addition, they enjoy a ready two-way market globally. These coins are manufactured at the national mints of various countries—West Point (the United States), Winnipeg (Canada), Pretoria (South Africa), Vienna (Austria), and Perth (Australia)

With some exceptions, gold bullion coins trade at most retail firms at 5% to 7% over the gold price. This premium above the gold price consists of wholesale markup, retail markup, and seigniorage. Seigniorage is a charge the mint places on the coin to cover manufacturing costs and profits. It usually averages in the 2.5% to 3.5% range. Wholesalers add about 0.5% to 1%. Retail brokers and dealers usually add commissions from 1% to 3%, depending on the size of the order and other factors.

Along with standard one-ounce coins, most mints also manufacture gold coins in smaller denominations of one-half, one-fourth, and one-tenth ounce. Because it costs approximately the same amount of money to manufacture any coin no matter the size, the smaller the coin the greater the premium per ounce. You can find current pricing in the financial sections of most local newspapers as well as in the national business and financial newspapers and at various Internet sites.

The South African Krugerrand—
The First Legal-Tender Gold Bullion Coin

The first legal-tender gold bullion coin to gain worldwide use in the modern era was the South African Krugerrand, introduced in 1967. To this day, many gold owners equate gold ownership with Krugerrand ownership. The Krugerrand was minted specifically to contain one pure troy ounce of gold so that its value was based on the international spot price of gold. Though it contains one pure troy ounce, its overall fineness is 0.9167, or 91.67% pure gold. Denominated as one ounce of gold, it is struck with no currency value indicated on the coin.

(Fineness refers to the pure gold weight per 1000 parts. A fineness of 0.9167, for example, translates to 91.67% pure gold. Fineness does not refer to the amount of pure gold within the coin, but instead to the overall purity. To conceptualize, if you were to put a Krugerrand on a scale, it would actually weigh about 1.1 ounces—1 ounce of pure gold plus base metal, like copper, intended to harden the coins against potential damage. Gold coin purity is also stated by karat weight. Pure gold is 24-karat, of course—.9999 fine or 99.99% pure, whereas 22-karat translates to .9167 fine or 91.67% pure. By way of comparison, 14-karat translates to .583 fine or 58.3% pure.)

Other Bullion Gold Coins

The concept of a one-ounce coin tied to spot gold's fluctuations quickly caught on. Canada made its entry in the competitive bullion gold coin market in 1979 with the Maple Leaf, the first pure gold bullion coin minted without alloy—a concept that quickly garnered a significant share of market interest, particularly in the Far East. In early advertisements, Maple Leaf coins were pictured flowing from a gold bullion bar—an artifice effectively making the point that bullion gold coins' pricing was related to the spot price.

In 1986, the U.S. Mint introduced the United States Eagle, and the Austrian Philharmonic quickly followed in 1989. The United States Eagle is the most popular bullion gold coin with American investors. Like the Krugerrand, it is also 0.9167 fine—though containing one ounce of pure gold. The Canadian Maple Leaf, as mentioned earlier, the American Buffalo, the Australian Kangaroo, and the Austrian Philharmonic, on the other hand, weigh one ounce and are 0.9999 fine, or 99.99% pure. As mentioned, the key factor is that all six of these coins contain the same one pure ounce of gold, although they may weigh more than one ounce in total. Therefore, pricing can be readily compared.

The Pricing of Bullion

Gold bullion coins are priced in the United States during the business day using the COMEX in New York as a price basis. COMEX is the leading exchange for gold futures and options in the United States. Prices are set on the floor of the exchange by open outcry. Those prices are then recorded electronically and relayed around the world via the Internet and various quoting services. The price changes constantly during the trading day. After closing, dealers base their pricing on the after-hours GLOBEX market price, which also fluctuates continuously. The GLOBEX market is an electronic continuation of the COMEX floor trading.

Some dealers allow their better customers to lock in prices over the telephone, but this usually requires that you have an established relationship with the dealer or broker. Some firms will take a credit card number to ensure your follow-through on the locked-in price. In lieu of locking in over the telephone, your dealer may require that good funds be on hand—by wire or cashier's check—before your purchase price is set. Upon receiving your funds, dealers will either execute your order at market or contact you before locking in the price, depending on your wishes. Differences between the amount you send and your actual price are then paid by check before actual delivery.

Bullion coins are available primarily at gold bullion firms and coin dealers. Banks and stock brokerage firms have largely withdrawn from this market in the United States, having found it difficult to make the two-way market investors require. Many European and Asian banks still make a two-way daily market in gold bullion coins.

Should You Buy Gold Bullion Bars?

Most experts recommend that investors avoid bullion bars. Although the commission and markups are marginally less on bars than on coins, complications come into play when the time comes to sell bullion. Most dealers will want to see the bars before they buy them because of problems with counterfeiting. Some will not buy without an assay, a chemical analysis that determines the gold's purity. In most cases, gold firms will not set the resale price until the bars have been delivered to their location or depository for inspection. This presents difficulties if the client is anxious to capture a price and finds out that it can't be done until after the buyer has received the bars. Similarly, bullion bars could also present problems for those wishing to trade gold for merchandise in the event of an economic breakdown, because the individual receiving the gold bullion has no way of knowing whether the bars are real or counterfeit.

Holding gold bars in depository accounts—a situation that arises with Individual Retirement Accounts (IRAs), other retirement and pension plans, or depository accounts held for trading purposes—circumvents the liquidation and assaying problem in most instances. If the gold never leaves the account, in other words, if the client does not take delivery, the metal usually can be liquidated without an assay. If the owner decides to take delivery, I generally recommend exchanging the bullion bars for gold coins as a way to facilitate future liquidation.

Because of these trade and exchange difficulties, I usually counsel buyers to avoid bullion bars. The marginal added cost on bullion coins is a small price to pay when weighed against the potential disadvantages of owning bars.

Accelerated Demand in Times of Financial Stress

Finally, demand for gold bullion coins can accelerate greatly during times of financial stress and economic uncertainty. For example, during the financial crisis of 2008 and 2009, the six national mints that produce the most widely sold gold bullion coins were running at full capacity to keep up with demand. The United States Mint instituted an allocation program to ration its production. U.S. Gold Eagle bullion coin sales to the public, as shown in Figure 6., were representative of the strong increase in bullion coin sales across the boards. Note the two time periods of strong sales coincided with the Y2K scare in the 1998–1999 period and during Wall Street's financial crisis in 2008–2010. Such spikes in demand serve as a warning to gold accumulators. Because the demand for gold bullion coins is global in scope, shortages can develop quickly in times of stress and drive premiums significantly higher. The best course of action is to purchase ahead of a crisis instead of in the middle of it. Take to heart the old saying that the best time to buy gold is when things are quiet.

From the time of Lydia's Croesus, who was the first to mint gold coins (and from whom the legend of the Midas Touch evolved), the coining of gold served to standardize weight and purity and thus to facilitate trade and commerce. Modern gold bullion coins are the descendants of the coins first minted by Croesus.

B is for Bullion Coins – The simplest, most direct way to own gold.

Figure 7. **Commonly Traded Gold Bullion Coins**

Austrian Philharmonic
2000 shillings
Gross Weight: 31.103 grams (1 troy ounce)
Fineness: .9999 or 24 karats
Diameter: 37 mm
Fine Gold Content: 31.103 grams (1 troy ounce)
Also available in $^1/_2$, $^1/_4$, $^1/_{10}$ troy ounces

American Eagle
$50
Gross Weight: 39.33 grams (1.0910 troy ounces)
Fineness: .916 or 22 karats
Diameter: 32.7 mm
Fine Gold Content: 31.103 grams (1 troy ounce)
Also available in $^1/_2$, $^1/_4$, $^1/_{10}$ troy ounces

Canadian Maple Leaf
$50
Gross Weight: 31.103 grams (1 troy ounce)
Fineness: .9999 or 24 karats
Diameter: 30 mm
Fine Gold Content: 31.103 grams (1 troy ounce)
Also available in $^{1}/_{2}$, $^{1}/_{4}$, $^{1}/_{10}$ troy ounces

Australian Kangaroo
$100
Gross Weight: 31.103 grams (1 troy ounce)
Fineness: .9999 or 24 karats
Diameter: 32.10 mm
Fine Gold Content: 31.1033 grams (1 troy ounce)
Also available in $^1/_2$, $^1/_4$, $^1/_{10}$ troy ounces

South African Krugerrand
No currency value
Gross Weight: 31.933 grams (1.0909 troy ounces)
Fineness: .9167 or 22 karats
Diameter: 34 mm
Fine Gold Content: 31.1033 grams (1 troy ounce)
Also available in $^1/_2$, $^1/_4$, $^1/_{10}$ troy ounces

Chapter 3

C is for . . .

Choosing a Gold Firm

Your choice of a gold firm can mean the difference between your success and failure as a gold owner. Choose the right firm and it will help you stay the course on protecting your assets from economic uncertainties. Choose the wrong firm and you can be easily diverted from true gold ownership to myriad related, but speculative and/or derivative, investments. High-end numismatics, leveraged precious metals accounts, graded contemporary bullion coins, off-brand bullion bars and jewelry items, gold stocks, precious metals futures contracts, and options or exchange traded funds (ETFs)– all have a gold component as part of their profile, but none are a substitute for physical gold coins and bullion that you own outright.

Only gold coins and bullion meet the four basic criteria for safe-haven status—*liquidity, portability, exchangeability, and appreciability*, if I might coin a term, in direct correlation to the international spot gold price. Inherently there is nothing wrong with owning any of the other investment vehicles listed above as long as you are mentally and financially prepared to shoulder the risks. If, however, your principal goal is to own gold for asset-preservation purposes, it follows you would be best served by a firm specializing in gold coins and bullion for delivery.

For the beginning investor, it pays to be cautious in choosing a gold firm because how strongly you start affects how you will finish. Creating a comfort zone in which you can make your gold purchases with a strong degree of confidence and safety should be your primary goal. A logical and commonsense approach would be to interview a few gold firms to find one that is a good fit.

Some of the basic guidelines for choosing the right gold firm follow.

Select an Established Firm

Attempt to find a gold firm that has a solid track record. Ten years in business is good; fifteen years or more is even better. During the course of this secular bull market, a good many opportunists have set up shop in the gold market. Many of these firms are no more than home-based operations with little to no experience in the gold market. Their websites, however, make them look every bit as appealing as some of the brick-and-mortar firms that have been around for decades.

How Long Has the Firm Been in Business?

How do you know if a firm is established? A good start would be to ask a simple question: How long have you been in business? Firms fifteen years old or more have been involved in the gold market through thick and thin. They have demonstrated, in both good times and bad, a commitment to the industry that carries a great deal of value to you as an investor. A firm tempered by experience can help you shortcut the overall learning curve so that you establish your core portfolio position quickly—an objective with distinct advantages in these uncertain times. In addition, a firm that has demonstrated long-term stability and accountability is likely to be around should you decide at some point to liquidate all or part of your holdings.

In addition, a firm that has been around for a while can also guide you over some of the hurdles commonplace to gold investors entering this market for the first time. It can answer your questions quickly, efficiently, and thoroughly, thus cutting the learning curve.

For most investors, what to buy becomes an important, if not the most critical, question. A good gold broker can put you on the right path after asking just a couple of simple questions:

- Why are you buying gold?
- What are you thinking about these days to prompt your looking into gold?

The broker who doesn't ask such questions is probably inexperienced, and lacks the prerequisite professionalism to put you on the right track with respect to your interest in gold ownership. Too often the gold clerk is interested in touting what the firm wants him to tout. An interest in you specifically as an investor is an indicator that you might have found a firm worth further investigation.

Find a Smart Firm

During your time as a gold owner, much is likely to change in the economic and political landscape. You will want to stay informed, and the mainstream press does not always report prominently on the trends important to you as a gold owner. Choose a firm with a commitment to presenting news and opinion with respect to the gold market and an interest in keeping you informed as a long-term gold owner. To this end, the better gold firms usually offer services like newsletters and sponsor information-based websites. When interviewing a potential broker, probe their knowledge and understanding of the economic processes at work in the gold market. A broker who is knowledgeable, professional, and engaged in your interests will be a far greater asset to you in the long run than one who performs essentially a clerking function.

Find a Company Interested in Hearing You Out

A firm that knows its business can help you choose the right portfolio mix to address your specific goals, circumstances, and concerns. Understand the difference between the "client-oriented" and "customer-oriented" gold firms. The latter generally compete on the basis of price with little or no attention paid to your particular interests or portfolio needs. A question like, "Why are you buying gold?" would never be asked because the objective is to fill the order and move on to the next transaction. You say you want gold coin X. They may sell you gold coin X, or Y for that matter, with little regard to how that choice might fit your overall diversification plan. Client-based firms are more interested in you as an individual, and what you are attempting to accomplish as a gold owner.

Beware of Aggressive Sales Tactics

Choose a company with a large and satisfied client base. You will benefit from the experience it has gained working with a variety of situations. The firm that is abrupt at the outset is likely to give you short shrift if you have a question or concern that needs to be addressed in the future. Be wary of companies that use aggressive sales tactics. If a firm calls you repeatedly, badgers you, or calls with one great deal after another, be careful. There might be something wrong. If they persist in trying to sell you something in which you have no interest or that doesn't fit your needs and goals, this is a red flag. Resist and seek more information and other opinions. Do not make a decision until you have received sufficient information. Above all else, seek out and develop a relationship with a firm that handles your inquiry in a friendly, professional manner.

Check Out the Company's Real Line of Business

The level of expertise in the gold market varies from firm to firm as does their general interest in the economy and financial markets. Although there are many outlets for gold, there are relatively few with staffs capable of providing reliable direction to the first-time investor.

What's more, not every gold firm touting its wares has asset preservation as its top priority. And then there's always the firm that totally disregards the individualized needs of the inquiring client and concentrates instead on its own agenda. Before you even contact a gold firm, it would serve your best interest to ascertain the real nature of its business. You can learn much by browsing a company's website—something even the smallest firms offer these days. If its product line, services, and, most importantly, its focus, seems a good match, a follow-up call is in order. If not, keep searching. The initial spadework will end up saving you considerable time, effort, and dollars over the long run.

Check Credentials through the Better Business Bureau

A firm that has proven itself trustworthy can help you avoid some of the problems, pitfalls, and wrong turns often encountered on the road to gold ownership. Choose a gold firm with good credentials and a solid history. It should go without saying that checking out a company should precede a purchase, but it is surprising how many people bypass this important step, and end up paying the price.

One reliable source is a Better Business Bureau (BBB) profile—something any reputable gold firm should have. (If it is not a member of the BBB, that is a red flag in itself.) Neither the Securities and Exchange Commission, nor the Commodities Futures Trading Commission or any other government oversight agency, regulates the physical gold business. Though imperfect, the Better Business Bureau remains one of the few impartial judges of a gold firm's reputation.

The BBB has gone to an online automated program that makes it easy to bring up a profile on any gold firm in which you have an interest. There you will find basic information—the company's BBB rating along with a history of complaints and how they were handled. A record of dissatisfaction, particularly if there have been a large number of complaints, can be a warning sign even if the complaints were settled satisfactorily. To maintain an A+ rating, a business must only settle its complaints. It does not have to alter its business practices to avoid such complaints in the future.

All in all though, the Better Business Bureau does a good job alerting consumers on the business practices of its members. BBB firms must adhere to a strict code of conduct and submit to arbitration in the event of a dispute. By doing so, members are granted the right to display the BBB Reliability Program logo. The Gold Star certificate—the BBB's highest accolade—goes to companies that have had no complaints filed against them over a three-year period.

Check and Compare Pricing

A well-positioned firm with strong industry connections can assure you that the prices you pay are in line with market expectations. When you compare prices, make sure that you are comparing apples to apples. Ask for quotes as a percentage over the gold price. With prices moving by the second, price comparisons cannot be done effectively any other way. Keep in mind that cheaper is not always better. In fact, below-market pricing is a bright red flag. If a deal sounds too good to be true, it probably is.

Trust Referrals

If you know of a friend or family member who has had a good experience with a gold firm and feels comfortable about referring it, that might be the best indicator of all and a valuable resource for you as a beginning gold investor.

Ask about Transaction Details

What does the firm recommend for asset preservation purposes? What does it recommend for speculative profit potential? How should the portfolio be balanced? When is the price set? Is it locked in while your payment is being sent? What premiums are you paying over the gold price? What forms of payment are accepted? How will your gold be shipped? Make sure that your metal is sent either registered and insured by the U.S. Postal Service, or fully insured by private carrier. In both cases, you want to be sure it is being sent "signature required."

Trust Your Instincts

If you go through this process, receive acceptable answers to your questions, and you like what you see and hear, go with that firm. If you have the slightest doubt, especially if the firm does not sufficiently meet the criteria above, then go back to square one and start over. Better to be safe than sorry.

Focus on Your Objective

Gold coins and bullion should primarily be viewed as a portfolio hedge and insurance against a variety of economic and financial uncertainties, an objective that should be secured before moving on to the risk and profit aspect of gold investing. If, at the outset, you find a highly professional gold firm, one that is not attempting to advance its own agenda, and one that is interested in helping you choose the right gold product mix for your portfolio and at the right price, go with it. Unbiased, objective advice from one's gold advisor is key to successful entry into the gold market.

C is for Choosing a Gold Firm – Do your due diligence. It is time well spent.

Chapter 4

D is for . . .

Diversification: Now More than Ever

Diversification—distributing one's assets across a spectrum of investment alternatives—is one of the hallmarks of prudent portfolio management. For most, diversification amounts simply to dividing one's available capital among stocks (including mutual funds), bonds, and cash savings. However, if gold is excluded, such a division of assets is superficial at best, because it fails to take into account the corrosive effects of currency depreciation and financial market stresses on the overall portfolio.

Former chairman of the U.S. Federal Reserve Alan Greenspan has made many favorable comments about gold over the years. Even when chairman of the Fed, he remained one of gold's most eloquent defenders, a position he has maintained for most of his life. The following comment, given during congressional testimony some years ago, goes to the heart of the issue with respect to gold's overall portfolio role:

> "I do think there is a considerable amount of information about the nature of a domestic currency from observing its price in terms of gold. It is a longer-term issue. It is an issue which I think is relevant, and if you don't believe that, you always have to ask the question why it is that central banks hold so much gold which earns no interest and which costs them money to store. The answer

is obvious: they consider it of significant value, and, indeed, they consider it the ultimate means of payment, one that does not require any form of endorsement. There is something out there that is terribly important that the gold price is telling us. I think that disregarding it is to fail to recognize certain crucial aspects of the value of currencies."

Why Buy Gold?

This brief but revealing statement from a man who, as Fed chairman, spent a good part of his day worrying about currency values illustrates the importance of gold in portfolio diversification, for private investors as well as central banks. As a matter of fact, if you were to ask a hundred gold buyers why they own gold, a respectable majority would answer simply: "For diversification." Most investors equate diversification with peace of mind. It implies preparation for a variety of potential economic events. If the portfolio is properly structured, it matters not if stock markets crash, bonds lose value, or currencies suffer debasement. The hard assets of the portfolio will pick up the slack.

Swiss money managers, renowned for their ability to handle money and who manage investments for some of the world's wealthiest people, traditionally recommend a diversification into gold of 10–20%, and for good reason. Beyond the normal risks of market fluctuations associated with stock and bond investments, there is the additional danger of depreciation in the currency underlying the stock or bond. Denominated in a domestic currency (pesos, yen, euros, and dollars), these investments rely on sound central bank and government currency management policies to maintain their value. It is conceivable that a corporation or municipality, for example, could be perfectly managed yet its bonds could still erode in value due to debasement of the currency in which it is denominated.

Adding Gold to Your Portfolio

Gold diversification makes particularly good sense when stock and bond markets have reached cyclical highs, even if the plateau extends over a period of months or years. In many cases (but not always), gold moves opposite the trend in equities markets. In the late 1990s, when the U.S. stock market was at an all-time high, many investors began to move out of stocks and bonds and into gold with the hope of securing profits garnered in those markets. This strategy paid dividends a few years later when gold shook off its long dormancy and began to rise. Those who failed to diversify saw many of their stocks plummet—some disastrously—although the Dow Jones Industrial Average (DJIA) itself stayed range-bound. In the United States today, gold diversification is viewed generally as a commonsense portfolio strategy, and millions include it as part of their investment planning.

For American investors the decade of the 2000s, one that featured a bear market in stocks, serves as an interesting case study for the power of diversification in an overall investment portfolio. The graph (Figure 8) shows two model portfolios during the 2000s, one invested 100 percent in stocks, and the other invested 70% in stocks and 30% in gold. Each portfolio started with $100,000 in the year 2000. The all-stocks portfolio kept pace with the diversified portfolio until 2002, when both stocks and gold began to react to various aspects of the burgeoning debt crisis. By 2003, the diversified portfolio, for the first time, modestly outperformed the all-stocks portfolio as gold entered into the first stages of its bull market.

Eight years later in 2007, the all-stocks portfolio had managed to eke out gains just below 20%, while the diversified portfolio had chalked up gains just below 80%. After the collapse of Lehman Brothers in 2008, the gold diversified portfolio was worth almost double the value of the all-stocks portfolio ($152,000 versus $81,000).

Figure 8. **Portfolio Diversification Study: All Stocks versus 70% Stocks/30% Gold**

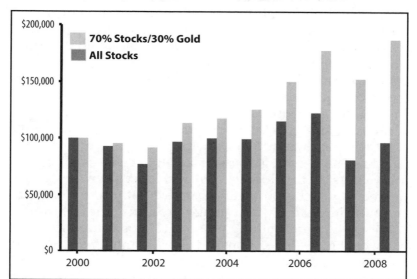

The Dow Jones Industrial Average closed December 31, 2000, the first year of the new century, at 10,787. By the end of 2009 it was trading at 10,428, having moved sidewise for most of the decade, with the exception of the crisis year 2008 when it lost roughly a third of its value. Gold started the new century at $273 per ounce and was trading at $1088 per ounce at the end of 2009—a gain of nearly four times over the decade. In 2008, while the stock market languished, gold retreated to the low $700s but quickly returned within weeks to its average price for the year at about $870 per ounce. In doing so, it convincingly proved once again its mettle as a crisis hedge. As 2009 progressed, gold once again broke above the $1000 per ounce mark and by year's end had gone through the $1200 per ounce barrier—a new all-time high.

Figure 8 amply illustrates the power and value of proper diversification. Gold in the modern era, although it is described, classified, and utilized in many different ways, is still first and foremost portfolio insurance and should be viewed as such. Simultaneously, it is rarely offered by traditional investment houses, so it is atypical for the suggestion to add gold to your portfolio to come from your financial advisor. Investors who feel traditional standard investment house strategies fail to fully insulate against volatile investment markets would be well served to become proactive about gold ownership on their own. Too often the suggestion to diversify into gold never comes up, and your portfolio ends up looking like the all stocks option featured in our study.

I recommend a gold diversification of 10–30% of your total assets, not including your residence. Obviously, the degree to which you diversify between those two figures is a function of how you gauge prospects for the overall economy. A good starting point is 10% of your assets, just in case. From there, your level of commitment should move incrementally higher to match your level of concern, to a maximum of 30%. During the 2000s, a commitment of 30% in the overall portfolio more than compensated for the negative effects of a bear market in stocks, bonds, and the dollar.

D is for Diversification—Diversify and let the winds of economic uncertainty carry you where they may.

Chapter 5

E is for . . .

Education: The Key to Successful Gold Investing

Truth must be ground for every man by himself out its husk, with such help as he can get, indeed, but not without stern labor of his own
—John Ruskin

In a book like *The ABCs of Gold Investing*, the sole purpose of which is to provide an education for those contemplating gold ownership, it might seem a bit superfluous to devote a chapter to the merits of becoming educated. After all, you would not be reading this book if you did not want to become more educated on the subject. In past editions, I emphasized that the reader should take the time to become informed and stay informed as an important part of one's portfolio planning. Various resources and services were listed where that might be accomplished along with a note of encouragement. In this edition, rather than revisiting what has now become familiar ground in the burgeoning information age, I thought it might be useful to utilize the ongoing financial crisis as an educational tool—an event from which we can draw, through "stern labor," some important lessons of our own.

"Why Didn't Anyone See This Coming?"

When the financial crisis of 2008 began to take its toll on the United Kingdom, Queen Elizabeth famously asked the question: *"Why didn't anyone see this coming?"* The question was directed at the London financial community, but the same could have been asked of the mainstream media, academia, or the regulatory apparatus of the government. Queen Elizabeth's more public quandary aside, for countless investors on both sides of the Atlantic Ocean the question took on a more personal tone: "Why," they asked their financial advisors, "wasn't I advised that this might be coming?" Had they been honest with themselves, the question would have been reduced to something more elemental: "Why didn't I see this coming?"

After all is said and done, each of us is responsible for the stewardship of our own portfolios, and to blame anyone else is pretty much an exercise in both futility and passing the buck, especially when it comes to matters as all-inclusive as the state of the economy. The Queen of England's concerns are wider than our own, that is, the welfare of the nation. We, on the other hand, can safely narrow the scope to our own financial well-being. The universal answer to the question was the one the Queen first received: "No one saw this coming." The implication, of course, was that if no one saw the financial crisis coming, then no one reasonably could be held accountable—a response that comes off to the attuned ear more like an excuse and an inadvertent warning than a suitable explanation.

Had Queen Elizabeth asked her question in the right circles, she might have received another answer entirely because, in reality, there were a great many who saw the financial crisis coming. John Paulson, the redoubtable hedge manager, saw it coming. In fact, he made a massive bet on the real estate crash via a security especially created for him by Goldman Sachs, the Wall Street investment bank. Paulson's bet netted billions in the housing bust. Michael Lewis, in his best-selling book, *The Big Short*, tells the story of four investment fund managers who saw it coming and reaped substantial rewards. Michael Lewis himself saw it coming and tried to warn others.

No doubt other, less visible fund managers and investment advisors can claim similar prescience. In fact, I warned of the possibility of a financial breakdown in both earlier editions of this book (1996, 2005) and suggested gold as a sound hedge. The professional money managers and analysts, like John Paulson and Michael Lewis, were joined by thousands, perhaps millions of individual investors who recognized the potential for a breakdown. Among these many insulated themselves by hedging their portfolios with gold. The one trait all of these people held in common was a healthy skepticism that allowed them to separate themselves from the herd and strike out on their own.

The Perils of Unmitigated Positive Thinking

Similarly, in the late 1990s and early 2000s, too many investors forgot that a healthy skepticism was part and parcel of a successful approach to the market. Unfortunately, that loss of focus contributed to millions believing the utopian mantra that markets and the economy no longer cycled, that we were on a one-way street to perpetual prosperity, and that the stock market would never falter again.

Such unmitigated positive thinking cost investors trillions during the subsequent stock market meltdown and credit crisis. Even a cursory study and understanding of the financial markets and their history might have encouraged a more pragmatic portfolio approach. After all, the history of financial cycles in reality is just as rich in mania, panics, and crashes as it is in bull market triumphs, although only a handful on Wall Street would have subscribed to such anecdotal evidence during the first decade of the twenty-first century.

Too often, the investor finds a comfort zone that blunts the intellect. Bad news is to be avoided, as is the disagreeable opinion. A false optimism replaces both common sense and the healthy skepticism mentioned earlier. People believe because they want to believe, not because the belief has any basis in rational thought. They listen but they do not hear. In short, emotion overrides intellect, and whenever that happens, market losses are sure to follow.

In the aftermath of the 2008 financial crisis, Alain de Boton wrote an essay for the *Financial Times* titled "For a happier life, shake off your optimism." In it he said: "It is time to recognise how odd and counter-productive is the optimism on which we have grown up. For the last 200 years, despite occasional shocks, the western world has been dominated by a belief in progress, based on its extraordinary scientific and entrepreneurial achievements. On a broader perspective, this optimism is a grave anomaly. Humans have spent most of recorded history drawing a curious comfort from expecting the worst. In the west, lessons in pessimism have derived from two sources: Roman Stoic philosophy and Christianity. It may be time to revisit some of these teachings, not to add to our misery but precisely so as to alleviate our sorrow."

He goes on to quote the Roman stoic, Seneca: "You say 'I did not think it would happen.' Do you think there is anything that will not happen, when you know that it is possible to happen, when you see that it has already happened?" "Seneca," says de Boton, "tried to calm the sense of injustice in his readers by reminding them—in A.D. 62—that natural and man-made disasters will always be a feature of our lives, however sophisticated and safe we think we have become."

These are not the thoughts of a pessimist, but of a realist. During the course of the year prior to the writing of this chapter, an earthquake and tsunami struck Japan with devastating consequences, including a nuclear reactor meltdown; riots erupted in several Middle East countries; a war was fought in Libya; the Greek economy and banking system collapsed; a sovereign debt crisis shook Europe to its foundations; and, the United States and France lost their triple A credit ratings. There is little doubt that Seneca was right. In the end, there is as much justification for preparing for the worst as there is for the best.

Fed chairman Ben Bernanke made a similar point to Seneca's in a speech before the Council on Foreign Relations in March of 2009:

> "Financial crises," he said, "will continue to occur, as they have around the world for literally hundreds of years. Even with the sorts of actions I have outlined here today, it is unrealistic to hope that financial crises can be entirely eliminated, especially while maintaining a dynamic and innovative financial system. Nonetheless, these steps should help make crises less frequent and less virulent, and so contribute to a better functioning national and global economy."

One need not live life with a cloud constantly hanging over one's head. At the same time, an unwarranted optimism, as de Boton suggests, can lead to unfortunate results. A well-grounded, realistic attitude covers the middle ground and suits the times in which we live.

Lessons Learned from the Financial Crisis

Owners of gold or not, we have all received a practical education over the past decade under the tutelage of the ongoing financial crisis. A handful of investors weathered the crisis well, as pointed out in an earlier section of this chapter, but for too many it was an education delivered painfully in the school of hard knocks. Perhaps it was lesson enough. If, though, we gain nothing from the experience, the opportunity, and lesson, are lost. As Ben Franklin warned long ago, "Experience keeps a dear school, but fools will learn in no other."

What would those who surrendered to the notion of a Goldilocks economy (one not too hot, not too cold, but just right), and an eternally rising stock market, give to go back in time and reject that false assumption? Much suffering and financial loss could have been avoided. In retrospect, the choice between acceptance and rejection appears obvious, but it is in the heat of the moment that those choices really matter, and where the quality of one's education asserts itself.

Few of us have the time, or inclination, to acquire the necessary knowledge by taking a few classes at a local university, though there might be some wisdom to such an approach. At the same time, an occasional trip to the bookstore or the library, or continuing one's education by using the convenient, yet extensive resources offered on the Internet, would go a long way in closing the knowledge gap.

The challenge of the twenty-first century and the next phase of the Information Age will be to find, segregate, absorb, and utilize large amounts of information without losing focus on what is most important to you as an investor. The quality of the information you receive and your own analytical abilities in processing it will be the difference between success and failure.

Cultivate a realistic, pragmatic attitude about your future prospects. Simultaneously, educate yourself about the workings and history of the economy and the financial markets. Such self-reliance was the key to avoiding disaster in 2001 (the stock market correction) and 2008 (the credit/financial crisis), and it will likely be the key to avoiding disaster in any future financial meltdown.

E is for Education–Get one. It is the gateway to a secure financial future.

Chapter 6

F is for . . .

Fundamentals: Gold's Supply and Demand

Supply-and-demand tables are the kind of dry economic statistics that send people to the exits. But, before you fast-forward through this chapter, keep in mind that most experts believe the unusually strong supply-demand fundamentals will be the engine that drives the secular bull market in gold to its next level. To be sure, understanding and keeping abreast of the fundamental relationship between how much gold is being produced (the international supply) and how much is being consumed (the international demand) will be the key to making you an informed and confident gold owner, both now and in the future.

Many gold analysts now believe gold will exceed its previous high of $1895 (London P.M. Fix) per ounce sometime in the second decade of the twenty-first century. Some go so far as to predict prices of $2500 (Merrill Lynch's Sabine Schels) or even $3000 per ounce (Maisson Placements' John Ing and *The Economist's* Matthew Bishop) over the coming years, and I have seen predictions as high as $7000 per ounce (Bank of America's Macneil Curry). Such optimism is usually based not only on the burgeoning worldwide economic and dollar crisis (which is formidable in its own right), but also on a convergence of supply-and-demand factors as outlined below.

On both sides of gold's supply-demand ledger, the elephant in the room is China. It is the world's largest producer of gold as well as its second-largest consumer,

Figure 9. **Gold Price (1971–2011)**

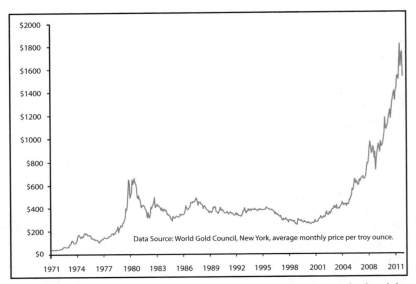

Data Source: World Gold Council, New York, average monthly price per troy ounce.

after India. Its central bank is an active, though highly secretive, buyer in the open market, and demand for investment items among its citizenry has grown exponentially coincident with its rapid ascent to the world's second-largest economy.

Gold Supply

The total supply of gold for 2011, according to the World Gold Council, was 3994 tonnes. Of that, 2809 tonnes came from the world's gold mines and 1612 tonnes came from recycled scrap. Two other categories that traditionally added to the supply—producer hedging and official sectors sales—have defected over the course of the last few years to the demand side of the fundamentals equation for reasons described below. Making up much of the gap left by producer hedging and central bank sales, recycled scrap has increased as a result of the significant rise in gold's spot price over the past several years. (The World Gold Council includes 2011 central bank demand of

440 tonnes as a negative figure in the supply section of its fundamentals table, thus making the data a bit confusing.)

Mine Production

Mining companies contribute to the supply of gold in two important ways—as producers of the metal itself through mining operations and in the forward market as sellers of the metal in advance of production.

According to the U.S. Geological Survey (2010 statistics), China, at 345 metric tonnes, is now the world's largest gold producer, supplanting South Africa, the nation that held that position for decades. Australia ranks second at 255 tonnes. The United States ranks third at 230 tonnes. Russia and South Africa are tied for fourth at 190 tonnes each. China's production has risen steadily over the past several years. U.S. production has declined steadily from about 300 tonnes in 2002 to 230 tonnes in 2010. Australia's production is spotty but generally in decline as well. South African production, it should be added, is declining rapidly. In 2002 it produced nearly 400 tonnes of gold. By 2010 that production had fallen to 190 tonnes—a decline of over 50%.

As mentioned earlier, the World Gold Council estimates 2011 mine production at 2809 tonnes and running at a relatively stable level for the past several years. Pierre Lassonde, former chief executive officer for Newmont Mining, explains why world mine production has remained steady despite record gold prices: "When is the last time we had a 30 million ounce discovery in the world? It's not in this decade; I can tell you that (and) it's not over the last 10 years. It's a long time ago. Look at exploration expenditures—they are going up, but we are not getting the discoveries. And not only are we not finding them, but the ones we do find, they take forever to put into production." Lassonde goes on to say that in his view "it's not going to get any better—at least for the next five years, and possibly for as long as the next 10 years."

For many years, the mining companies also affected the gold fundamentals by adding to the supply through selling their production forward. A forward sale involves two parties—a buyer and seller—agreeing on a transaction in advance of actual production, processing and refining of the metal.

As gold's bull market progressed, steadily rising prices made hedging an unprofitable practice. Mining companies, in turn, were encouraged, and in some cases forced by their stockholders, to steadily buy back their previous forward sales—a process called dehedging. For example, if a mining company had sold its gold production forward at $400 per ounce when spot gold traded at $600 per ounce, it would effectively be losing $200 per ounce—a circumstance likely to depress stock value. In order to keep its stock attractive to investors, the best strategy was to reverse forward sales, thus exposing production to the market price of gold. As for the supply-demand fundamentals, when a mining company dehedges, it abandons its previous role as a seller and instead enters the market as a buyer. The effect over the past decade has been dramatic. What was once *supply* that acted to restrain the price became unanticipated *demand* that drove the price higher.

Over the past several years, mining companies have slowly unwound their hedges, and in 2011 actually added 12 tonnes of new hedges to the supply side of the table. As we move through the second decade of the new century, repurchases are likely to continue playing a diminished role in the supply-demand fundamentals. At the same, mining companies will remain under pressure from stockholders, who typically prefer exposure to the international gold price, to contain or end forward sales. One, however, cannot completely rule out forward selling as a means to financing gold mining operations. Bank financing sometimes requires mining companies to lock in selling prices through forward sales in order to protect their loans from price erosion.

No discussion of gold's supply side would be complete without taking into consideration the fact that two of the top five gold producers—China and Russia—are engaged in government-sponsored purchasing programs from their domestic mines. The net effect of domestic purchasing programs is to keep supply off the market. China, as mentioned, is the world's top producer of gold and Russia ranks fourth. As a result of these direct purchases, between 400 to 500 tonnes of the world's annual production, or roughly 20%, never reach the commercial market, but make their way instead to those nation's reserves. Russia's central bank purchases about 75% of its miners' production; China's central bank, experts believe, now purchases almost all the gold produced within its borders.

This policy of building reserves through domestic production relates directly to their highly publicized concerns about the future value of the dollar and the stability of U.S. sovereign debt. It also draws attention to gold's traditional role as the universal store of wealth and final means of payment. The People's Bank of China is on record as advocating a target gold reserve of 4000 tonnes (it now holds about 1050 tonnes)—roughly half that of the United States, and nearly four times its current holdings. In other words, it is unlikely that China's mine production will reach the open market for many years to come.

Experts speculate that other producing nations might be encouraged, as time goes on, to follow China's and Russia's example. Says the World Gold Council, "[E]merging markets continue to build large external reserves, to provide them with security in the face of ever challenging market conditions. With the importance of gold universally reaffirmed by central banks, emerging country central banks are likely to continue purchasing gold as a means of preserving national wealth and promoting greater financial market stability. Central banks remain committed to the importance of gold and its relevance in maintaining stability and confidence as they have been for hundreds of years."

Official Sector (Central Bank) Sales

Central banks contribute to the supply side of the fundamentals equation in two important ways—through outright sales, and through the little-understood process of gold leasing, or lending.

Central Bank Gold Lending

Central banks lend gold through commercial institutions, often referred to as "bullion banks" that offer gold banking services. The five banks that set the London Daily Gold Fix—Barclays Capital, Deutsche Bank, Scotia Mocatta, the Hong Kong and Shanghai Bank Corporation (HSBC), and Societe General—are some of the largest and most active in the gold market. The Rothschild Group is still believed to play a role in the gold banking community though a lesser one since it resigned as chairman of the London Fix. Central banks lend gold to these (and other) institutions and receive an interest fee in return called the lease rate. The bullion banks in turn lend that gold to mining companies to fulfill their forward sales programs, and financial institutions that use the metal to finance other investment operations. In either case, the use of the metal entails selling it in the open market, a process that adds to the supply.

The net result is a lease pool of metal that rises and falls based on both market needs and the willingness of the central banks to lend out their reserves. The lending pool is not generally included in most supply-demand tables. It is notoriously difficult to accurately peg the amount of gold being leased by the central banks from year to year. Virtual Metals, the London-based analyst, is generally regarded as providing the best estimates. In 2004, it reported the gold-lending pool at 4315 tonnes. By 2008, in the wake of the first wave of the financial crisis, that figure had dropped to 2345 tonnes. For 2009, it estimated the pool to be 1862 tonnes—all in all a dramatic turnaround from the 2004 figure.

Figure 10 - Gold Supply-and-Demand Table, 2002–2011

In metric tonnes	2002	2003	2004	2005	2006	2007	2008	2009	2010	2011
Supply										
Mine production	2591	2592	2478	2550	2481	2447	2410	2589	2709	2809
Net producer hedging	-412	-279	-445	-86	-373	-400	-352	-236	-108	12
Total mine supply	2179	2313	2034	2464	2108	2047	2058	2353	2600	2822
Official sector sales	545	617	497	662	367	485	232	34	77	-440
Recycled scrap	835	944	829	886	1107	937	1316	1695	1641	1612
Total supply	3560	3875	3360	4012	3582	3469	3606	4081	4163	3994
Demand										
Fabrication										
Jewellery	2680	2522	2673	2707	2283	2426	2304	1814	2017	1963
Technology	291	318	348	431	458	465	461	410	466	464
Dental	69	67	68	-	-	-	-	-	-	-
Sub-total fabrication	3040	2907	3088	3138	2741	2891	2765	2223	2483	2426
Bar & coin retail investment	373	314	396	412	421	441	875	776	1199	1487
EFTs and similar	-	-	-	208	260	251	321	617	368	154
Total demand	3413	3221	3484	3731	3400	3547	3962	3617	4050	4067
OTC investment and stock flows	147	653	-124	280	182	-79	-356	464	113	-73
London PM fix (US$/oz)	309.68	363.32	409.17	444.45	603.77	695.39	871.96	972.35	1224.52	1571.5

Data Source: London Bullion Marketing Association, Thomson Reuters GFMS, World Gold Council. All figures are rounded.

Western Europe's central banks are the world's largest gold lenders at 873 tonnes. Asian central banks are second at 318 tonnes. The United States does not lend gold. It is no coincidence that the price of gold went from the $450 per ounce range to the $1100 per ounce over the same 2004–2009 period. The drop in the gold-lending pool directly affected the amount of gold available to the marketplace. This reduction in lending can be attributed to three primary causes—the Central Bank Agreement on Gold (CBGA), which capped the gold-lending pool (more on the CBGA later); stubbornly low lease rates, which discourage central bank lending; and the financial crisis itself, which encouraged central bankers globally to take a more cautious approach to their gold-lending activities.

Central Banks Net Gold Buyers
for First Time in Decades

The official sector globally, as a result of the ongoing financial crisis and concern about the dollar's role as a reserve currency, has become a net buyer of gold. Up until their dramatic collapse of sales in 2009, central banks' mobilizations had been a presence on the supply side of the fundamentals for decades. In 2000, net sales by central banks amounted to 479 tonnes, or 12% of the supply. By the end of the decade in 2009, that contribution had dwindled to 34 tonnes, according to the World Gold Council, or less than 1% of the total supply. In 2010, central banks' sales remained low, a mere fraction of what they were at the beginning of the previous decade, 77 tonnes. In 2011, for the first time in decades, central banks became net buyers of gold at 440 tonnes, a turnaround that stunned gold-market analysts.

By adding the 545 tonnes of *supply* in 2002 and converting it to 440 tonnes of *demand* in 2011, it amounts to a nearly 1000-tonne swing in the supply-demand picture. James Steele, an analyst for HSBC, summed up its meaning: "Since U.S. dollar foreign exchange holdings are already at record levels in many countries, we believe these nations will seek to increase gold reserves, in a bid to diversify their USD–laden reserves. While we do not expect official sector activity to move the market near term, *we regard central bank purchases as a bulwark of the long-run gold rally."* [Emphasis added.]

To What Do We Owe This Extraordinary Turnaround?

To fully understand the longer-term significance of the central banks' change in attitude about gold, we must first gain an understanding of their fundamental role in the past. In the process, we will gain a better understanding of gold's role in the international monetary system and why so many analysts, like Mr. Steele, believe that the change will underpin gold's bull market for a long time to come. Finally, it will also serve as an adjunct and natural bridge to the demand side of the gold equation.

Since the early 1960s, central banks have attempted, with varying levels of success, to impose their will on the gold market. In most instances that imposition was directed toward keeping the price in check either by selling the metal outright, as was the case in the 1960s and 1970s, or through a combination of sales and leases, as began in the late 1980s and extending through much of the 1990s. As such, this demonstrates the quantifiably inverse relationship between official sector sales and leases and the gold price. When an intervention (for lack of a better word) is in progress, the price is restrained. When it is abandoned, the price begins rising more quickly than it would under normal circumstances because of built-up price pressure.

This helps explain the various spikes on the gold chart in the past, including the one that began at the turn of the twenty-first century. Had the practice of aggressive selling/lending not distorted the market, gold's price increase may have been gradual and less dramatic as it would have been driven more by the normal interrelationship between buyers and sellers in a free market. Quite possibly, the run-ups that did occur, particularly the two spikes in the 1970s, would have been more subdued and stretched over a longer period of time.

Central bank intervention in the gold market came under scrutiny in the late 1990s, partially as a result of a series of gold auctions conducted by the Bank of England that depressed the price at under $300 per ounce. As a result, the Central Bank Agreement on Gold—a document regulating sales and leases of gold—was signed by a consortium of European central banks in 1999. It became a watershed for the gold market and the event many analysts point to as the catalyst for gold's long bull market.

The Central Bank Gold Agreement: A Watershed Event for the Gold Market

When central bankers representing the nations of Europe signed the Central Bank Gold Agreement in September 1999, George Milling-Stanley of the World Gold Council spoke for many in the gold industry:

> "It is important to recognize that the agreement represents something of infinitely greater significance than a mere repetition of statements central bankers had already made, or a clarification of positions they already held. This is a binding agreement, signed by central bank governors on behalf of their respective institutions and/or governments . . . This should finally put to rest the fear that has kept the gold market in its paralyzing grip for years, the fear that central banks have abandoned gold as a reserve asset, and are planning to sell all that they have... That fear flew in the face of all the observable evidence. It is a matter of fact that only five governments have sold a significant quantity of gold in the past 10 years, if we define a significant quantity as 100 tonnes or more."

The agreement, in fact, went much deeper than simply controlling central bank gold sales; it also curtailed the leasing of gold and central bank involvement in the futures and options markets. Haruko Fukuda, at the time Chief Executive Officer for the World Gold Council, spoke eloquently on the subject at the Denver Gold Group conference that year:

> "On Sunday 26th September—just three weeks ago—a new era dawned for gold. For the first time in almost exactly 28 years, since convertibility of gold into U.S. dollars for official holders was suspended on 15th August 1971, the governments with the largest gold holdings made a positive joint statement on gold. Those three decades have been a period in which gold was persistently sidelined by the official sector attempting to demonetize gold. In recent years the market has been plagued by persistent rumors of ever increasing official sector sales and each and every announcement of sale by central banks has acted as a trigger for a new downturn in the price of gold. Yet the amount of gold held in reserve by the official sector has barely declined during that period—a decline of a mere 6% in three decades."

To be sure, as Ms. Fukuda spoke, gold was trading in a range around $300 with many calling for it to go below $200. Within three years, its descent was broken and its long rise had begun.

The Central Bank Gold Agreement was simple, but direct:

1. Gold will remain an important element of global monetary reserves.

2. The above institutions will not enter the market as sellers, with the exception of already decided sales.

3. The gold sales already decided will be achieved through a concerted program of sales over the next five years. Annual sales will not exceed approximately 400 tonnes and total sales over this period will not exceed 2,000 tonnes.

4. The signatories to this agreement have agreed not to expand their gold leasing and their use of gold futures and options over this period.

5. This agreement will be reviewed after five years.

Signatories to the agreement were: the European Central Bank, and the central banks of Austria, Belgium, Finland, France, Germany, Ireland, Italy, Luxembourg, the Netherlands, Portugal, Spain, Sweden, Switzerland, and the United Kingdom. The Bank of Japan, although not a signatory, publicly endorsed the agreement the following day. The U.S. Federal Reserve, also not a signatory, also endorsed the agreement. (Neither the United States nor the International Monetary Fund lend gold.)

In March 2004, the signatories renewed the agreement for an additional five years with one changed provision: They increased the amount of gold to be sold over the five-year period from 2000 to 2500 tonnes, a relatively benign change. In 2009, the agreement was renewed for another five years with minor changes.

The effects of the Central Bank Gold Agreement had an important psychological impact on the international gold market, as Haruko Fukuda predicted. No longer could the specter of gold sales be held like the sword of Damocles over the gold market. It set the stage for the second most dramatic event in the contemporary history of the gold market—demand from the world's central banks and emergence of strong investment demand on a global basis.

I will leave you with one more thought with respect to the supply of gold before we move on to the demand side of the equation. The ultimate question with respect to the central banks' exit from the gold market as sellers is: "How is the supply gap left by their exit going to be filled?" At the moment, that gap is filled by recycled scrap, but there is no guarantee jewelry box liquidations, whether in the East or West, will proceed as they have in the past.

Gold Demand

The demand side of the fundamentals table encompasses three large categories (2011 statistics): jewelry and other fabrication at 1963 tonnes, or just over 48% of the total (4067 tonnes); investment at 1641 tonnes (154 tonnes in exchange traded funds) or just over 40% of the total; and technology at 464 tonnes or just under 11% of the total. Official sector purchases amounted to 440 tonnes. An interesting oddity to gold's current fundamentals is that the same forces driving gold on the supply side are driving it on the demand side—a protracted economic crisis, a fundamental change in the psychology governing the activity of producers and consumers, and a general recognition of gold's role as the ultimate store of value.

Fabrication Demand

In the Far East and South Asia, a large portion of the market for jewelry fabrication is considered a safe-haven investment. In fact, the spreads between the buy and sell on gold jewelry in India for example are very narrow, implying a strong two-way market. For this reason, it is difficult to separate jewelry as a monetary asset from that which is used for adornment. In general, worldwide jewelry demand since 2005 has weakened somewhat as the price has risen. Even so, it remains the largest single component and continues to underpin the demand side of the gold ledger. When prices decline, demand tends to rise, and vice versa. As such, it has become something of a constant, a backdrop against which the rest of the demand side of the equation operates. Technology demand consistently runs in the 350 to 400 tonnes range.

Investment Demand

The World Gold Council reports that investment demand totaled 1641 tonnes for 2011 (including exchange traded funds [ETF] demand)—a high point for the past decade. Of that amount, 1487 tonnes were purchased in the form of coins and bars—a nearly 25% increase over 2010. Europe, amid a sovereign debt crisis that threatened to topple its banks and monetary system, led the world in the purchase of coins and bars at 267 tonnes. India ranked second at 217 tonnes and China third at 180 tonnes. The United States purchased nearly 106 tonnes in coins and bars in 2011. Exchange traded fund volumes went from 368 tonnes in 2010 to 154 tonnes in 2011—a 58% drop. Obviously, by a wide margin, coins and bars remain the preferred form of worldwide investment, even though ETFs recently garnered much publicity due to the involvement of major hedge funds and Wall Street firms. A remarkable aspect of the record growth in retail demand globally is that it occurred during a time of general worldwide *disinflation* belying gold's reputation as strictly an *inflation* hedge. Investors' fears about the safety of banks and financial institutions contributed significantly to the record growth.

Tocqueville Funds' erudite John Hathaway explains how strong and rising gold investment demand could very well be with us for some time to come:

"There are two reasons to invest in gold. First, there is the simple and obvious prospect that it may rise in price and thereby create positive returns for those of us who hold it or gold mining shares. The second reason is not quite so obvious, but it is more powerful. It is the fact that gold's behavior is uncorrelated to other financial assets including bonds, stocks and currencies. When expected returns on financial assets are low, money flows in the direction of gold. It is also true that gold, being uncorrelated as opposed to inversely correlated, can rise while financial asset prices are also rising. It is these characteristics that qualify gold as a form of financial insurance. . .The bull market in gold is well underway. While it will suffer periodic setbacks, it will not reach its completion until world governments restore integrity to financial instruments beginning with paper money. There is little to suggest that such a moment is within view."

Conclusion

Gold's fundamentals are to be digested with an eye to the long-term. The most important exercise in analyzing the fundamentals for gold, or any other market, is attempting to identify the trend. That is why the experts spend so much time analyzing the underlying forces driving the market. As shown earlier, it took nearly three years for the effects of the Central Bank Agreement on gold to be reflected in the price. In the short run, the gold price is driven, if not dominated, by the market for what we call "paper gold" in the trade—futures, options, and even exchange-traded funds. Once you understand the nature of the trends and how they might affect the price over the long run, you will find yourself a more secure and confident gold owner.

Now you have a basic understanding of the market fundamentals that make the gold market tick. This brief outline of a very complex subject is in no way meant to be a comprehensive analysis of the supply-and-demand fundamentals of gold. Whole volumes have been devoted to such an analysis. For the previous edition of this book, I concluded this chapter by saying "accelerating demand and decelerating mine production combined with curtailed central bank involvement on the supply side presents an opportunity unlike anything that has occurred in the gold market since the United States abandoned its interventionist gold policies in the 1970s." For this edition, I would simply say that not much has changed since then, except the trends seem even more favorably and deeply entrenched than when those words were written. The stubborn nature of the ongoing international financial breakdown and its effect on private citizens and governments alike will continue to weigh heavily in gold's favor on both sides of the supply-demand ledger for years to come.

F is for the Fundamentals—Understand the interplay between supply and demand and build your long-term confidence as a gold owner.

Chapter 7

G is for . . .

The Great American Bailout: More the End of the Beginning than the Beginning of the End

By the end of 2008, America sensed that its chickens had come home to roost. Instead of learning from past mistakes, though, the nation's leaders appeared intent on compounding them. The massive bail, rescue, and print operation conjured up to address the subprime credit crisis was simply a continuation of the same policies that brought about the crisis in the first place—more debt, more easy money, more moral hazard, more taxpayer responsibility, and more government intervention. Only now these programs were being carried out on a far grander scale than ever before. At some point in the future, the consequences are likely to arrive on a far grander scale as well.

According to the *New York Times*, the federal government has committed $9 trillion for bailouts of financial institutions, industrial corporations, and quasi-government agencies like Fannie Mae and Freddie Mac. It has committed an additional $1.7 trillion to insure financial institutions and another $1.4 trillion as a direct lender to banks. In total, the government is on the hook for $12 trillion in commitments, of which about $2.5 trillion has actually been spent. That figure does not include the $700 billion Troubled Asset Relief Program (TARP).

While the government was busy bailing out the corporate and financial sector, the Federal Reserve was busy bailing out the federal government to the tune of $1.7 trillion in direct purchases of U.S. Treasury securities. In addition, the Fed committed another $1.1 trillion to purchases of mortgage-backed securities from commercial banks. In other words, the financial crisis of 2008–2009 quite literally was papered over with the largest liquidity blizzard in American history. Indeed, the chickens had come home to roost but, as you are about to read, for all the roosting, all we have gotten for our trouble is more chickens.

In its wake, the greatest bailout in economic history would leave a lingering sense of unease at the junction of Wall Street and Main, a feeling that perhaps the other shoe was about to drop. Banks continued to fail, almost on a weekly basis, and the Federal Deposit Insurance Corporation (FDIC) continued to bail them out. By early 2012, there were still 813 banks on the FDIC's problem list.

The Federal Reserve, adding to this sense of unease, continued to soak up, in one way or another, much of the financial sector's otherwise unwanted paper in its quantitative easing program—a policy many believe will deliver inflationary consequences down the road. The federal government, for its part, continued to go into the hole at the rate of some $5 billion a day and $1.3 trillion per year. The national debt, the final repository for everything that is not collected in taxes by the federal government, stood at a little over $10 trillion at the beginning of the crisis, and at nearly $15 trillion by the end of 2011.

The Consequences of the Great American Bailout

Long before the financial crisis and the European sovereign debt crisis became dinner table conversation, the United States had established itself as the greatest debtor nation on earth. Mervyn King, the governor of the Bank of England, not known for making blunt or

Figure 11. **Federal Government Debt, Total Debt**

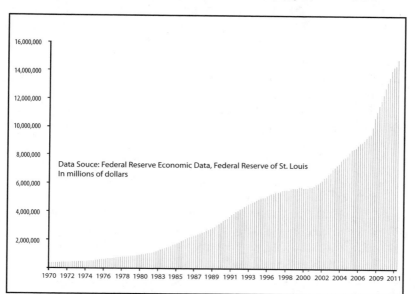

controversial statements, remarked that the United States, the world's largest economy, was just as much immersed in a sovereign debt problem as Greece or, for that matter, other countries in Europe including the United Kingdom. "[O]ne of the concerns in financial markets," said King, 'is clearly—how will this enormous stock of public debt be reduced over the next few years? And it's very important that governments, both here and elsewhere, get to grips with this problem, have a clear approach and a very clear and credible approach to reducing the size of those deficits..." Of course, as the governor of the Bank of England, he well knows there are only three resolutions to any debt—pay it, default on it, or, in the case of the national government with the benefit of a fiat money system, inflate it away.

The United States enjoys an advantage over other nation-states in dealing with its debt and deficits. Its currency happens also to be the world's primary reserve currency. This distinction provides a ready market for its debt issue, resulting in significantly more leverage and latitude than any other nation-state on earth. The United States has enjoyed this unique debt-financing advantage since the end of World War II. Charles DeGaulle's finance minister, Valerie Giscard d'Estaing, once called it America's "exorbitant privilege."

Dr. H. J. Witteveen, former director of the International Monetary Fund, explained the mechanics of the exorbitant privilege like this:

"This system (the fiat dollar standard) can be criticized, because foreign exchange reserves are created as a consequence of balance of payment deficits of the United States without any relationship to world reserve needs. Implicit in this is an unfair advantage to the reserve country, the United States, because it can finance its deficits by paying in its own currency. This makes it too easy to run deficits, and it creates an inflationary element in the monetary system, compared to the classical gold standard... By paying in its own currency, the United States could continue to finance enormous deficits without being forced to introduce adequate deficit reducing measures."

And so, as a result, the U.S. national debt grew month after month, year after year, until it became—because so many countries own so much of it—an enormous shared burden for the world economy. Even before the 2008–2009 financial market meltdowns, some nation-states had begun questioning to what degree they should hold U.S. debt paper in the face of the massive fiscal deficits being run by the U.S. government.

In the aftermath of the crisis, the public criticism by America's creditors had translated into action. Japan, the number two creditor, had begun to slow its purchases of U.S. Treasury paper. China, the lead creditor, actually began reducing its holdings, ramped up its domestic gold production to circumvent the dollar reserve problem, and announced in 2010 that it had doubled its gold reserves over the previous five-year period. This shift in sentiment, combined with the huge funding increases resulting from the financial bailouts and two overseas wars (Iraq and Afghanistan), raised America's sovereign debt problem to a new level of global awareness. It simultaneously raised the specter of massive debt monetization—the contemporary equivalent to running the printing press— as a means to financing the government's deficits.

The Option to Print Money

Central banks that operate under a fiat money regime, like the U.S. Federal Reserve, are not likely to idly stand by and watch their financial system implode, the economy crash, or their government slide into a sovereign debt default—not if they can help it. Instead, they will employ whatever mechanisms are available to avert disaster. The policy options range from simple open-market operations, usually intended to lower interest rates and inject liquidity into the banking system, to monetizing federal government debt in the absence of traditional sources of financing, or to direct bailouts should they be required.

As Greece's sovereign debt problem came to a head in early 2010, Iceland's finance minister, Steingrimur Sigfusson, seemed pleased that his country had its own currency and its own central bank. Asked about the situation in Greece, he remarked, "Oh my God, I wouldn't want to be in the position they're in. The position Greece is in is quite different from the position Iceland is or was in; Greece has the euro and we can debate whether or not that's good for them for the time being." Iceland at the time was having financial system problems of its own. The difference between the two revolved around the issue of sovereignty—particularly economic and monetary sovereignty. Iceland had it. Greece did not. Iceland had policy options. Greece did not. Iceland could devalue its currency and buy time by inflating, or printing money. Greece was forced by its Euro-partners into a painful austerity program.

Monetization, as economists call it, is the sophisticated modern equivalent of an inflationary process first introduced in ancient times by the Roman emperors in financing their debts. They would take Roman aureus gold coins into the Treasury as tax payments, shave some gold off the edges, remelt the shavings, and mint them into more coins. The debased coins and the already circulating original coinage would then be used in transactions as equivalent in value. The quantity of gold in circulation had not increased, but the number of aurei had. Because an increasing supply of aureii was chasing roughly the same amount of goods and services, the net result was one of the first forms of currency inflation.

Likewise, inflation in the contemporary fiat money economy (and by using the word, "inflation," I am using the classical definition—"an increase in the supply of money and credit") is not so much an event as it is a process. The government goes into debt. To whatever extent it cannot finance the debt by selling it to a willing buyer, it monetizes by selling debt paper to the central bank. The federal government then spends those funds like it would any other, thus inflating the money supply. Eventually that inflation of the money supply translates to price inflation, just as it did in the case of the Roman aureii.

In 2003, amid the rising specter of deflation, a then relatively unknown Federal Reserve Board member by the name of Benjamin Bernanke caused a stir in financial circles with the following observation:

> "Like gold, U.S. dollars have value only to the extent that they are strictly limited in supply. But the U.S. government has a technology, called a printing press (or, today, its electronic equivalent), that allows it to produce as many U.S. dollars as

it wishes at essentially no cost. By increasing the number of U.S. dollars in circulation, or even by credibly threatening to do so, the U.S. government can also reduce the value of a dollar in terms of goods and services, which is equivalent to raising the prices in dollars of those goods and services. We conclude that, under a paper-money system, a determined government can always generate higher spending and hence positive inflation."

With that comment, Bernanke let the cat out of the bag years before he was ever elevated to chairman of the Federal Reserve. It was a hint of what was to come. When Bernanke alluded to the "printing press...or its electronic equivalent," he was referring to debt monetization. In an ironic manifestation of foreshadowed events, this same Benjamin Bernanke, as chairman of the Federal Reserve, would come to preside over the greatest bailout in contemporary American economic history, precisely by cranking up the printing press.

Charting the Great American Bailout

The following three charts (Figures 12, 13, 14) offer a snapshot of the Great American Bailout as a balance sheet item for the Federal Reserve System. By the end of 2011, the Federal Reserve under the rubric of "quantitative easing" had added over $2 trillion to its balance sheet in the form of Treasury paper and mortgage-backed securities—by far the two largest components—plus a long list of lesser bailouts in various forms. At the end of 2007, mortgage-backed securities were not a line item on the Fed's balance sheet and federal agency debt was listed at zero.

The first chart, Federal Reserve Bank Credit (Figure 12), encompasses all the categories considered "quantitative easing" including U.S. Treasury paper, federal agency paper, and mortgage-backed securities. The reader also should keep in mind that these additions

Figure 12. **Reserve Bank Credit, 1990–2010**

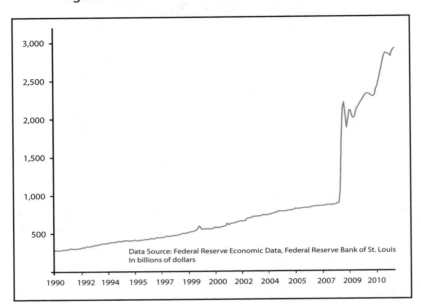

Data Source: Federal Reserve Economic Data, Federal Reserve Bank of St. Louis
In billions of dollars

to the Fed's balance sheet are separate from the federal government's bailout operations conducted through the Treasury Department and the Federal Deposit Insurance Corporation. It is also separate from normal funding operations sponsored by the Fed, such as rock-bottom interest rates and commercial bank borrowing at the discount window.

The second chart, Federal Debt Held by Federal Reserve (Figure 13), is a subcategory of the reserve bank credit chart. This component of the Fed's balance sheet represents the federal government debt held by the Federal Reserve System. Since 1970 this component has risen steadily and predictably, except for two periods in and around the crisis itself. The first was in 2008 and early 2009 when the member banks were in pursuit of liquidity and U.S. debt paper was the best candidate for quick conversion to cash. The paper was liquidated, thus the trough on the chart. The second period is the

Figure 13. **Federal Debt Held by the Federal Reserve**

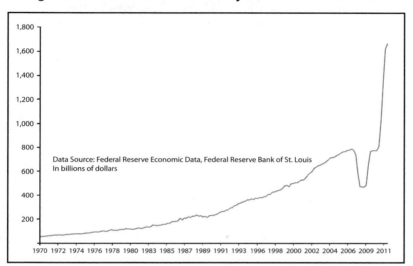

Data Source: Federal Reserve Economic Data, Federal Reserve Bank of St. Louis
In billions of dollars

rocket trajectory shortly thereafter, resulting from the Federal Reserve's *direct* purchases of debt from the U.S. government, that is, monetization. The purchases were a result of the federal government's huge funding needs coupled with reduced interest on the part of America's former creditors, as explained earlier.

What the future might hold as this dynamic plays out over the years to come is an open question. Because the Obama administration is already on record as stating the enormous $1 trillion-plus deficits could last for a decade or more, the only hope is for the other side of the equation—revenues—to work in the U.S. government's favor. If global creditors do not materialize as buyers of U.S. debt, this trend could continue and perhaps compound, making it important to monitor closely in the months and years to come. At this writing, the Federal Reserve System, not China as so many believe, is the largest holder of U.S. federal government debt. It holds $1.7 trillion in Treasury paper while China holds $1.1 trillion.

The situation with mortgage-backed securities (Figure 14)—the paper the Federal Reserve purchased from stressed

Figure 14. **Mortgage-Backed Securities Held by the Federal Reserve: All Maturities, 2002–2011**

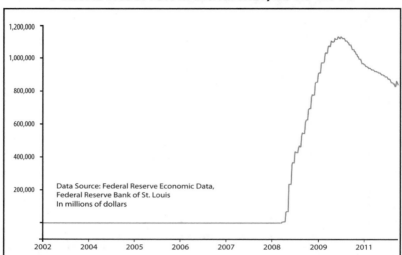

commercial banks—is another trend worth monitoring into the future. In 2008–2009 it constituted a sudden and massive addition to the Federal Reserve's balance sheet and an indirect and ongoing form of monetization. It peaked at roughly $1.1 trillion in 2010 and then tracked back during 2011 to the $800 billion level. Vice president of the St. Louis Federal Reserve, Daniel Thornton, in a paper titled "Monetizing the Debt" writes, "[I]f the Fed is holding $1.25 trillion in MBS (mortgage-backed securities) formerly held by the private sector, the credit previously supplied to the MBS market by the private sector is available to purchase government debt. Hence, as long as the amount of credit supplied by the private sector is not affected by the Fed's actions, the implications of the Fed's actions for federal finance will be much the same as if the Fed had purchased government securities—*a central bank does not have to purchase government securities to monetize debt.*" [Emphasis added.]

The Fed, through the New York Federal Reserve, did in fact create the money out of thin air to purchase the mortgage-backed securities from the commercial banks. The commercial banks in turn had, and still have, the option of loaning those funds to its customers—businesses and individuals—or the federal government. According to a *Forbes* magazine article ("Banks still binge on Treasury debt," 4/20/10), the banks in large proportion chose, at least in the beginning, to finance the United States government, instead of U.S. business or the consumer. From September 2008 through the end of 2011, the amount of Treasury debt held by the U.S. commercial banks, according to the St. Louis Federal Reserve, rose by about $550 billion—a not insignificant sum when you take into consideration that over the same period the Federal Reserve itself directly purchased another $1.2 trillion in federal debt securities. The total from the two operations comes to $1.75 trillion and constitutes the largest single monetization of federal debt in U.S. history.

Returning to Thornton's brief analysis, "The monetary base (currency plus reserves) is called 'high-powered money' because each dollar of reserves can support multiple dollars of bank deposits that are included in various monetary aggregates like M1 and M2." The good news is that this process tends to keep interest rates low as well as the government in business. The bad news is that, because all of this ends up on the Fed's balance sheet as part of the monetary base, it could also run-up the money supply and fan the inflationary fires at some point down the road. Too, the monetization process creates a dangerous form of moral hazard for the government itself. As long as the federal government relies on printed money to make ends meet, whether through the Federal Reserve directly or by a more circuitous route through the commercial banks, it avoids the messy business of balancing the budget. It also perpetuates an ongoing dependency on the money-printing process.

Often overlooked in considering the full effects of the Fed's massive purchase of mortgage-backed securities

Figure 15. **The Monetary Base Versus the Gold Price, 1984–2011**

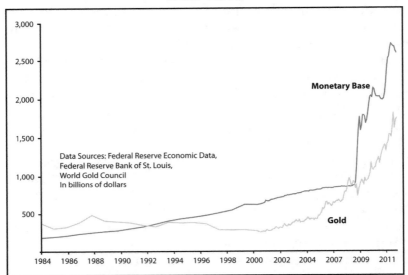

is the fact that the Federal Reserve could have a difficult time draining liquidity from the system down the road should it decide to tighten. In the past, it would simply sell treasuries to the commercial banks to drain reserves, drive up interest rates, and tamp down inflation. Selling questionable mortgage-backed securities to commercial banks (already happy to get them off their balance sheets) as a means of draining liquidity might prove to be problematic—a circumstance that would frustrate Fed policy, or lead to other, possibly more damaging, policies when the time comes to tighten credit.

Ultimately though, for our purposes in determining the effects of the Great American Bailout, the Fed's purchases of mortgage-backed securities and federal debt land on its balance sheet as part of the monetary base. Growth of the monetary base, in turn, is directly correlated to future inflation and the price of gold (Figure 15). If the monetarist school is correct about the lag times between stimulus and effect, these particular chickens should come home to roost beginning sometime in 2012 to 2013.

On the other hand, it could turn out that the money that has been created thus far goes only to fill some very large holes in the economy, and perhaps it ends up accomplishing that and nothing more. Economist Andy Harless asks the question, "Will monetizing the Federal Debt cause inflation?" then answers it with "only if we're lucky." As the answer implies, though, failure to do so might result in something even worse. The fact of the matter is that no one knows for certain how this experiment in monetary policy is going to end and that, in and of itself, is an argument to own gold—a store of value versatile enough to cover the range of possibilities.

G is for the Great American Bailout: To paraphrase the great British statesman, Sir Winston Churchill, it is more the end of the beginning than the beginning of the end.

(Final note: Though this chapter focuses its attention on quantitative easing in the United States under the auspices of the Federal Reserve, it should be noted that by March 2012, similar programs had been launched by the European Central Bank, the Bank of England, and the Bank of Japan. The prospects for global inflation were elevated as a result.)

Chapter 8

H is for . . .

Historic Gold Coins:
Perhaps Necessary, but
Not Necessarily Expensive

Investors who are concerned about the possibility of a government gold call-in or seizure often include historic gold coins from the mid-nineteenth and early twentieth centuries as part of their gold ownership plan. A short review of gold's history in the 1930s Depression era explains the legal rationale that underlies this strategy.

In 1933, when the Franklin D. Roosevelt administration closed the banks, seized gold bullion by executive order and banned its ownership, it also exempted gold coins "having a recognized special value to collectors of rare and unusual coins." In 1954 the Treasury Department broadened that definition to specify that "all gold coins minted prior to 1933" were subject to the exemption. A subsequent regulation in 1962 went a step further by allowing the importation of all gold coins minted before 1933 as collectors' items. That chain of events clarified the definition of "rare and unusual coins" and established the precedent for similar treatment in the event of a future call-in or seizure, although such treatment cannot be guaranteed. Few people know that between 1933, when it became illegal to own gold bullion, and 1975, when ownership privileges were restored, investors could own gold coins dated before 1933 because of this exemption.

Today, there is a large international two-way market for these items. Some of the more commonly traded coinage

Figure 16. **Commonly Traded Historic Gold Coins**

United States of America
$20 Gold Piece
Liberty Design
Gross Weight: 33.346 grams
Fineness: .900 or 21.6 karats
Diameter: 34 mm
Fine Gold Content: .9675 troy ounces

United States of America
$20 Gold Piece
St. Gaudens Design
Gross Weight: 33.346 grams
Fineness: .900 or 21.6 karats
Diameter: 34 mm
Fine Gold Content: .9675 troy ounces

France
20 Francs
Rooster
Gross Weight: .207 troy ounces
Fineness: .900 or 21.6 karats
Diameter: 21 mm
Fine Gold Content: .1867 troy ounces

Switzerland
20 Francs
Gross Weight: .210 troy ounces
Fineness: .900 or 21.6 karats
Diameter: 21 mm
Fine Gold Content: .1867 troy ounces

Great Britain
Sovereign
Gross Weight: .2567 troy ounces
Fineness: .917 or 22 karats
Diameter: 22.05 mm
Fine Gold Content: .2345 troy ounces

France
Napoleon
Gross Weight: .207 troy ounces
Fineness: .900 or 21.6 karats
Diameter: 21 mm
Fine Gold Content: .1867 troy ounces

Netherlands
10 Guilder
Gross Weight: .2163 troy ounces
Fineness: .900 or 21.6 karats
Diameter: 22 mm
Fine Gold Content: .1047 troy ounces

Germany
20 Mark
Gross Weight: .2560 troy ounces
Fineness: .900 or 21.6 karats
Diameter: 22.5 mm
Fine Gold Content: .2304 troy ounces

in this genre are the British Sovereign, the Swiss 20 Franc, the Netherlands 10 Guilder, the German 20 Mark, and the French 20 Franc. (See Figure 16). During World War I the gold standard broke down in Europe, and most nation-states ceased minting gold coins. The United States did not go off the gold standard until 1933, at which time it also ceased coining gold money (Figure 16).

Commonly traded European coins from this period sell at modest premiums over contemporary bullion coins. They track the price of gold and enjoy good liquidity throughout the industrialized world. United States gold coins generally, but not always, sell for higher premiums than their European counterparts. U.S. gold coins do not necessarily track the gold price, but trade at prices set day to day by various national market makers.

Both U.S. and European gold coin premiums expand or contract depending on economic conditions as well as the ebb and flow of worldwide demand. Sometimes those changes can be significant—particularly during times of economic stress. Generally speaking, though, the premiums are relatively stable, and they tend to radically move out of their ranges only during times of economic instability and/or high demand. During the 2008 financial crisis, for example, premiums for European coins roughly doubled over previous levels.

The subject of a possible gold seizure has always been a controversial one among gold owners and advocates with equal fervor displayed on either side of the issue. A Google search under "gold seizure" produces a long list of links to articles on the subject, most of which center around its possibility, probability, and likelihood. Only a handful of searches express the opposite view, that is, that seizure is something gold owners should not be worried about. Investors, however, are not as interested in the political debate surrounding the issue, as they are in the practical business of protecting their assets in a worst-case scenario.

At a London conference sponsored by the *Financial Times* in 2010, John Levin, a managing director for the Hong Kong Shanghai Bank (HSBC), told the story of several top asset managers in the United States who control "massive amounts of capital," asking at a seminar conducted by the bank if large amounts of gold could be stored in Europe. When Levin asked why they wanted to store in Europe over the United States, the response came "that they feared that at some stage the U.S. administration might follow the path set by Franklin D. Roosevelt in 1933 and confiscate all U.S. holdings as part of the country's strategy in dealing with the nation's economic problems." I pass this story along only because it illustrates that these kinds of concerns permeate all levels of the gold market—from small private investors to fund managers who own billions of dollars in gold bullion and exchange-traded funds. HSBC is one of the five bullion banks that sets the London Daily Gold Fix and is a key player in the international gold market.

I should add that the word "confiscation" is often misinterpreted to mean seizing of property without just compensation. The Fifth Amendment to the Constitution, the so-called "eminent domain" clause, states that private property "cannot be taken for public use without just compensation."

There is an important caveat I would like to pass along. If you decide to include historic gold coins in your planning, make sure that you are not paying an excessive premium. Some gold-marketing companies, often those with high-profile national advertising campaigns, charge excessive premiums to cover their advertising costs. Too often investors mistakenly believe that the gold firm that sponsors their favorite political commentator on television or radio is also the best place to make their gold purchases. That is not always the case. In some instances, these gold-marketing companies charge as much as 50% or more over melt value for historic European gold coins—a premium substantially higher than what you would pay at a reputable gold firm.

David Ganz, J.D., a former president of the American Numismatic Association and authority on precious metals and numismatic law, puts it this way, "FDR's presidential seizure of gold specifically exempted 'rare and unusual coin.' That didn't mean 'expensive,' and it was not a synonym for 'pricey.'" Ganz defines the "rare and unusual" exemption along the lines described earlier in this chapter. The date of the gold coin, not the rarity or numismatic premium, is the chief determinant.

I view a new ban on gold ownership as a possibility, rather than a probability, and see historic gold coins, if properly approached, as a cost-effective hedge for those looking to address those concerns in their gold holdings. In most instances, the low additional cost involved in opting for these items under normal circumstances should not be a barrier—particularly if their inclusion in your portfolio provides peace of mind. If, however, you are not concerned about a gold seizure, then contemporary bullion coins or bars will get the job done for you.

By way of a final disclaimer, this chapter is not intended to be a formal legal opinion, but rather an overview to help you form your own opinion on whether or not historic gold coins should be included in your portfolio plan. For a formal legal opinion, I suggest you consult with your attorney.

H is for Historical gold coins – A diversification within a diversification.

Chapter 9

I is for . . .

The Inflation-Deflation Debate: More to It than Meets the Eye

Multiple-choice question:

Where do you stand in the inflation-deflation debate?

A. The Federal Reserve fails to kick-start the economy. As hard as it tries, it cannot get businesses and individuals to borrow and spend money. The unemployment rate rises to unheard of levels. Bankruptcies quickly follow. The economy sighs, and then tumbles into the *deflationary* abyss.

B. Years of quantitative easing, debt monetization, 0% interest rates, and mega-billion-dollar public bailouts finally kick-start the economy. Business picks up. Employment and consumer spending rise in a new era of good feeling. The economy rumbles, and then takes off on an *inflationary* tear to double-digit levels overnight.

Perplexed? Join the club. But, in order to totally "confuse" you, let me add a few more options:

C. The economy continues to limp along in a more or less featureless fashion as it has for most of the 2000s. Banks struggle. The financial system sputters. Business is generally subdued. Inflation remains moderate. Stubborn unemployment rates persist. The Federal Reserve continues to combat the malaise with easy money and a zero-interest rate policy. The economy stumbles along in a *disinflationary* mode.

D. Double-digit price increases combine with a double-digit unemployment rate. Concerns begin to surface that the economy might spiral into either an inflationary blow-off or deflationary crash. The Fed walks a tightrope between fighting inflation and encouraging growth. Instead of inflation or deflation, we get a blend of both—*stagflation.*

E. The Fed's easy-money policies begin to take their toll. The inflation rate begins to rise—slowly at first, then more rapidly. The Federal Reserve's attempts to stop the inflation fail, and fail miserably. Before long the inflation rate is running at triple digits, then quadruple digits. The economy superheats. The oft-predicted nightmare *hyperinflation* begins.

You get the picture. We live in a complicated world. As you see, inflation and deflation are only two options in a confusing range of possibilities. But here's the good news: Gold, because of its historic asset-preservation qualities, protects against any or all of these eventualities.

During a *deflation,* the general price level would be falling by definition. How the authorities might decide to treat gold under such circumstances is an open question. If subjected to price or currency-style controls, gold would likely perform the same function it did under the 1930s deflation—remaining fixed in value as prices fall. If free to float (the more likely scenario), the price would most likely rise as a result of increased demand from investors hedging systemic risks and financial market instability, as was the case globally during the 2008 financial sector meltdown.

During an *inflation,* gold rises along with the price of everything else. In most instances, because of the ramped-up demand, it rises faster than the rest of the commodity complex, thus providing a natural hedge. There is little dispute about gold's historic store of value function during inflationary episodes.

Up until the disinflationary 2000s, the manual on gold read that it performed well during inflations and deflations but not much else. As the decade of asset bubbles, financial institution failures, and global systemic risk progressed, gold continued its march to higher ground year after year, and it became increasingly clear that the metal was capable of delivering the goods during *disinflation* as well.

The United States experienced a near runaway *stagflation* in the 1970s. The period coincided with the first gold bull market of the post-1971, fiat money era.

During *hyperinflation*, gold is one of the few effective defenses. Those who weathered Germany's nightmare inflation in the 1920s did so by owning gold. In 1922, gold sold for 86.8 marks per ounce. So sudden and virulent was the hyperinflationary onslaught that, by the end of 1923, this same ounce of gold sold for 63.0168 trillion (paper) marks.

History shows that gold, better than any other asset, protects against the conditions described above. *Inflation, deflation, disinflation, stagflation,* and *hyperinflation*—it matters not. Gold protects against any or all and no matter in which order they arrive.

I is for the Inflation-Deflation debate—Buy gold and let others worry about what's next for the world economy.

Chapter 10

J is for . . .

Jump-Starting Your Portfolio Plan through Gold Ownership

The rich old speculator Bernard M. Baruch forehandedly bought gold and gold shares after the 1929 Crash. Years later a suspicious Treasury Secretary asked him why. Because, Baruch replied, he was "commencing to have doubts about the currency." Many are beginning to doubt the strength of the dollar, as they well might. Following Baruch's example, they should lay in some gold as a hedge.
—James Grant, *Grant's Interest Rate Observer*

Essentially, there are two broad categories of gold investors: those who want a safe haven to hedge disaster, and those who simply want to make a profit. A third type of investor seeks to combine both objectives. Your needs will determine what you include in your portfolio. Some thought and attention must be given to which of the three categories you belong. Along these lines, if you place yourself in the hedge disaster category, you must also determine which economic disaster you consider most likely to occur—inflation, deflation, or any of the rest of the economic maladies described in the previous chapter. What you conclude in this respect will play a determining role in how your portfolio should be structured.

Portfolio planning is inherently a very personalized business. It cannot be achieved without strong input from the client. Do your homework. Know what you want to accomplish. It is very important to making wise gold-investing decisions. To plan your portfolio properly, consult with a professional in the gold business. Stockbrokers, financial planners, mutual fund sales personnel, and the like have little knowledge of the highly specialized field of physical gold ownership. As a result, they sometimes confuse more than help.

Safe-Haven Investors

Those oriented toward hedging disaster generally prefer a combination of gold bullion coins and historic gold coins. The customary split is half of each. The bullion coins will protect your portfolio against currency deterioration, inflation, deflation, bank failures, stock and bond market collapses—the gamut of financial evils. What they won't protect you against is intervention in the gold market by the federal government, including capital controls or a potential seizure, or gold call-in, as occurred in the United States in 1933.

For an extra layer of protection against government intervention, you will want to include the historically significant European and/or lower-grade uncirculated United States $20 gold coins minted during the nineteenth and early twentieth centuries. Although complete protection cannot be guaranteed through the ownership of pre-1933 gold coins (in the United States, gold ownership is a privilege, not a right), precedent does offer a strong argument in their favor as historically relevant items. (See Chapter 8, "H is for Historic Gold Coins.") These items track the gold price and usually trade at moderate premiums over what you would pay for contemporary bullion coins.

If you rate the possibility of a new gold ban as low, then you should weight your portfolio in the direction of bullion coins—anywhere from 60% to 100%. If you are concerned about seizure and other forms of government intervention (such as capital controls), you should weight your holdings in the direction of the historic pieces—anywhere from 60% to 100%, depending on your level of concern.

Speculative Investors

Those who approach gold primarily for its profit potential generally stick with the gold bullion coins because of the low premiums, narrow spreads, and ease of liquidity. Thought should be given, however, to the white metals as well—silver, platinum, and palladium—but these are highly specialized markets that must be analyzed separately for their potential. Each is subject to its own set of supply-demand fundamentals.

Keep in mind that silver, platinum, and palladium are primarily inflation hedges—although with silver, as you are about to read in the next chapter, that assumption is undergoing change. They do not perform well in deflationary or recessionary economies when industry experiences a general slowdown. If you wish to pursue a speculative approach to gold and other precious metals, you should decide your portfolio composition under the guidance of an expert who can review with you the merits of each investment, and offer practical guidance on the best methods for storing and facilitating your purchases and sales.

Combining Safe-Haven and Speculative Investing

If you wish to combine safe-haven and speculative investing, the process becomes a little more complicated. You will need to decide various portfolio weightings. Timing also becomes an issue. You will need some combination of historic gold coins, gold bullion coins, and/or silver, platinum, and palladium bullion bars or coins to achieve this objective. Additionally, you should review the merits of each investment with a professional advisor, and then determine on your own how your portfolio should be structured, utilizing the guidelines herein as a template.

Miscellaneous Portfolio Concerns

If you think you might need to use gold as money, you should add one-fourth-ounce bullion coins and/or historic gold pieces that contain approximately one-fourth and one-fifth of an ounce of gold. These versatile gold coins fulfill two functions: utility as a form of money, along with the protection as historic items mentioned earlier. An alternative or addition would be the $1000 face-value bags of pre-1965 silver coins that contain 715 ounces of silver and trade relatively close to the spot silver price.

If you wish to hedge both inflation and deflation simultaneously, gold is your best bet. As mentioned in a previous chapter, gold tends to rise as the currency depreciates in inflationary times. In deflationary times, it tends to at least hold its value as the price level drops on most other items, thus preserving the gold owner's purchasing power. At the same time, some analysts argue for much higher gold prices during deflation simply because gold is one of the few investments that would survive a massive debt default and bank panic. Such a scenario would generate unprecedented demand, which would drive prices higher. If you feel inflation is the most likely future scenario, silver and platinum should be added to the mix.

Know Thyself

Defining your particular goals and needs before buying your first ounce of gold is a critical elemental to a successful portfolio approach. With that in mind, a few words are helpful concerning the mind-set with which you pursue your interest in gold and precious metals ownership. Some enter the gold market to make a profit, others to hedge disaster, some to accomplish both. Irrespective of which category you fit, make sure you understand why you are going into the gold market. Convey that understanding to the individual with whom you are structuring your gold portfolio. The *whys* have quite a bit to do with *what* you end up owning.

Frequently, investors will say that any kind of gold will do because "after all, gold is gold, isn't it?" This type of attitude has helped a great many coin-shop owners unload unwanted inventory they had not been able to get rid of for years—art bars, commemorative coins, bullion manufactured by little-known refiners, and so forth. Knowing yourself and knowing what role you would like gold to play in your portfolio goes a long way toward making you a happy, confident gold owner and avoiding the bumps along the road to gold ownership.

J is for Jump-Starting Your Gold Portfolio Plan— There's no time like the present.

Chapter 11

K is for . . .

Kindred Metal—Silver

No discussion on gold investing would be complete without at least a few words about gold's kindred soul—silver. For years, silver was shuttled to the back burner as an essentially industrial metal, the primary driver of which was industrial demand. However, silver's price performance during the disinflationary period after the turn of the twenty-first century leads many to believe that something is going on with silver that some analysts are missing. In 2003, the year gold broke out of the $300.00 range and began its trek higher, silver broke out of the $4.50 range and began to move with it. Since then, silver reached an interim peak in 2011 at nearly $46.00—outperforming gold by a wide margin. Over that period, industrial usage of silver remained in a range, while coin and investment demand quadrupled. Needless to say, this points to the public viewing silver as hedge in very much the same way it views gold, thus resurrecting the old idea of silver being the poor man's gold.

It used to be that silver was viewed as a commodity first and monetary metal second. Now it is being accumulated for monetary purposes as well, and much of the discussion in this book about gold's role as a long-term store of value can be applied to silver as well. The rap on silver has always been that it might not do well under deflationary circumstances. Now that notion has come into question due to its strong performance during disinflationary circumstances that have been very similar to a deflation—a time when investors' primary concerns center around the safety of bank deposits and the financial system in general.

Nevertheless, silver will continue to play a secondary role in most investment portfolios simply because of the difficulties encountered in its storage and transportation. Silver is a bulky investment. Even at current prices, moving $100,000 worth of the metal is an effort, and its owners often complain about the difficulty of preparing large amounts of silver for shipment when they wish to sell. This limits its usage among those who like to have their metal stored nearby.

More and more, though, investors are utilizing storage programs with well-known depositories to circumvent the shipping and storage problems. This gives the investor the opportunity to speculate on the price and move in and out of ownership positions with a phone call. The metal is kept in an allocated account in the customer's name. Account owners pay fees that cover insurance and storage, but those costs are relatively minor. In addition, most depository programs offer the option of taking delivery if the owner so desires. Because of the same problem with assaying and potential tampering or counterfeiting encountered in gold bars, I usually recommend that the owner convert to silver one-ounce coins before taking delivery to facilitate future resale and individual consumer transactions, if needed.

The price history of silver has been substantially more volatile than that of gold, with upsides as well as downsides much more pronounced. A correct call could help you end up with more profit than if you had purchased only gold to begin with. A bad call though could cost you dearly. Be forewarned. By way of illustration, when gold climbed from the $320.00 level to $430.00 in 2003–2004, silver went from roughly $4.50 to over $8.00. It then dropped precipitously back to the $5.50 level in a matter of weeks. Gold's downside was much less

Figure 17. **Silver Price, 1982–2011**

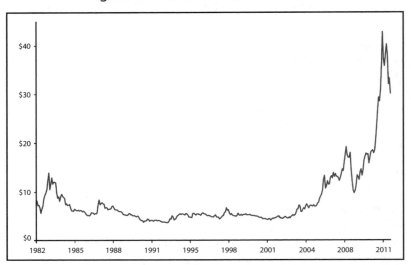

dramatic, bottoming near $380.00 As you can see, with silver, timing is everything. You would not have wanted to be one of the investors who bought into the market at $8.00 and have been forced to sell out at $4.50.

Supply-and-Demand Fundamentals

According to statistics supplied by the Silver Institute, silver production is spread evenly over a large number of countries: Mexico produces roughly 17.5% of the annual supply; Peru, 16%; China, 13.5%; and Australia, Poland, Chile, the United States, and Canada are all in the 7% to 8% range. Mine production has risen steadily overall since 2001, when 606 million ounces were produced. In 2010, 736 million ounces were mined. These production figures are likely to continue rising in future years. Silver production is primarily a by-product of gold and copper mining. If higher prices are in the cards for those metals, then expect silver production to rise. Scrap reprocessing is also an important component of the supply.

Presently, the main uses for silver are industrial (55% of supply), jewelry/silverware (25%), and photography (8%). Photographic usage has dropped dramatically since the 1990s from roughly 200 million ounces per year to just over 70 million ounces. However, the category of coins and bars for investment purposes has risen from 30 million ounces to over 100 million ounces.

Another 178 million ounces—an important number—needs to be added as implied investment for 2011. In 2004, implied investment was only 29 million ounces, according to the Silver Institute. Silver has turned in an impressive performance since the last edition of this book, and that performance has been driven largely by investment demand—a circumstance worth noting.

K is for Kindred Metal, Silver—Get richer with poor man's gold.

Chapter 12

L is for . . .

London, New York, Hong Kong, and Zurich: A Day in the Life of the Gold Market

Real gold is not afraid of the fire of a red furnace.
—Chinese proverb

Even as you read this section, a gold price is being posted somewhere in the world. Like the old British Empire, the sun never sets on the gold market (Figure 18). For centuries, gold has captured the imagination of those with a trading mentality, who dare to buy here and sell there with the hope of making a profit in the bargain. Now with the advent of computer screens, satellite transmissions, and instantaneously e-mailed buy/sell confirmations, the gold market has been internationalized.

It is not unusual for a trader in New York to take a position on the London market as he eats breakfast, and then sell that position in Hong Kong or Singapore as he prepares to retire in the evening.

London Market

For American gold traders, the day begins in London. Before traders on the East Coast have had their first cup of coffee, the five members of the London gold market have agreed on their morning gold fix. They have assessed supply and demand for that day. They have also established a price they believe will adequately match the buys and sells streaming in from mining companies, bullion

Figure 18. **A Day in the Life of the Gold Market**

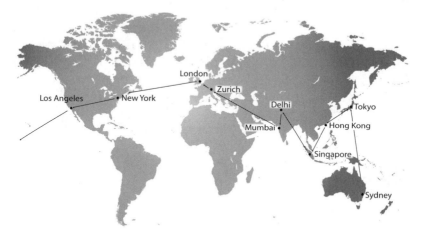

dealers and traders, central banks, internationally based commercial banks, refiners, and commercial brokerages. If the buys exceed the sells in sufficient quantity, the price is raised. If vice versa, the price is lowered.

In recent years, London has become an increasingly important center for the gold trade, making headway toward its old place at the head of the gold trading table—a place that both COMEX in New York and Zurich have lost. The reasons? London is where the world's leading banks and the bullion banks have set up shop for their gold deposit, lending, and derivative operations. London is home to the London Bullion Market Association that trades very high volumes in both physical gold and paper over-the-counter transactions.

Terry Smeeton, who once headed the gold and foreign exchange operations for the Bank of England, estimates that the volume in London is 7.5 million ounces daily. The London market offers both spot and forward sales. Spot sales represent gold sold at the posted London price. Forward sales represent gold sold by contracts in the future at an agreed-upon price, with the London market serving as the go-between. The five men who set the London fixes represent the largest, oldest, and most influential banks and gold dealers in the world: Barclays Bank (which provides the group's chairman), Societe General, the Hong Kong Shanghai Bank (HSBC), Scotia Mocatta, and Deutsche Bank. They set two fixes each day. The first, at 10:30 London time, is known as the A.M. Fix. This is the one usually announced on American radio networks as you commute to work in the morning. The P.M. Fix is set after lunch. All business is conducted strictly under the London Code of Conduct for bullion dealers over dedicated telephone lines set up exclusively for the five participating banks.

New York Market

The less-than-polite gold trading pit at the COMEX in New York opens at 8:20 A.M. Eastern Time and begins operations while the London market is still open. The highly charged auction atmosphere of COMEX stands in stark contrast to the restrained, dignified arrangement in London. We have all seen the COMEX video clips: frantic traders shouting at each other, waving their arms, pointing fingers, making hand signals—a picture of seeming confusion and anarchy. Interestingly, throughout the apparent chaos runs a thread of perfect order. Buys and sells are actually matched and prices set.

Typically, traders in the pit are young men and women for an obvious reason: the frenzy takes its toll. After the terrorist attack of September 11, 2001, which struck at the heart of New York's financial district, the trading day was shortened. The COMEX gold market now closes at 1:30 P.M. Eastern Time. From 1933, when President Franklin D. Roosevelt issued his executive order seizing Americans' gold, until 1975, when President Gerald Ford signed legislation re-legalizing it, gold did not trade formally in the United States. With gold's re-legalization, interest from the public and the financial community grew rapidly. COMEX moved to meet that interest with its popular 100-ounce futures contract. From the 1970s to present, COMEX became the dominant price-setting market. London now challenges that dominance but has yet to supplant it.

COMEX operates on a spacious trading floor in the World Financial Center in downtown Manhattan. The price generated on the trading floor is the one flashed on trading screens across the United States and around the world, and is used by gold firms as a base for pricing bullion and bullion coins. With the advent of the Internet, those prices are available by subscription in either real or delayed time, to which most brokers and traders refer continuously during the business day.

"COMEX price" and "New York price" are terms often used interchangeably by many gold firms. After COMEX closes, after-hours futures trading is conducted via the GLOBEX electronic trading platform. GLOBEX trading begins at 2:00 P.M. (ET) Eastern Time, Monday through Thursday, and concludes at 8:00 A.M. (ET) the following day. Trading starts for the week on Sunday at 7:00 P.M (ET).

Hong Kong Market

The next big market to trade is Hong Kong, and its pricing is reflected in the GLOBEX quotes. The Hong Kong market is venerable in itself, having first traded gold in 1910, when British banks thought they might need a mechanism for trading gold in the Orient. Today it is the launch site for gold going to mainland China, one of the fastest-growing gold markets in the world. In fact, the whole Asian market has been so active in recent years that American and European gold traders who travel there talk about it in the wistful tones normally reserved for the American market of the late 1970s and early 1980s.

This market is highly influential in Asia, because Hong Kong is where Japanese investors, banks, and financial houses occasionally hedge their orders and make their physical purchases. It is also in a time zone that fits nicely with the business day of traders in Saudi Arabia and the rest of the Persian Gulf, particularly the new and rapidly growing market in Dubai. If Hong Kong gold is moving, it is quite often due to buying or selling of the Middle East investors. Large amounts of Hong Kong gold are also made into jewelry for export throughout Asia. For the most part, Hong Kong serves as a convenient midpoint in the trading day because it fills the gap between markets in the United States and Europe.

In *World of Gold*, gold historian and analyst Timothy Green characterizes the Hong Kong market this way:

> "They (the Hong Kong traders) like awkward tael-weight bars (based on 1.2–ounce units) and resist suggestions that they should trade in ounces and U.S. dollars to conform to world patterns. They delayed for years the introduction of the Reuters monitor computer system, fearing a computer must invade the secrecy of their 'society.' For many American and European gold owners, these sentiments do not sound foreign at all."

Zurich Market

The next market to open in gold's day is Zurich, Switzerland. This market is dominated by the big Swiss commercial banks. They first made a splash in the world gold market by convincing South Africa that they would be better merchants for its gold than London, particularly since the Swiss banks would themselves be the end buyers instead of acting as intermediaries like the London banks. Then, in the early 1970s, Russia—at the time the second-largest producer of gold after South Africa—began to ship its gold to Switzerland. Zurich in this way became the largest dealer of physical gold bullion in the world, shipping to all corners of the globe.

Now, as Timothy Green puts it, "Gold is as much a part of Switzerland as the Alps and skiing." Switzerland appeals to a great many of the world's private sector gold-holders, the superwealthy who keep a significant portion of their assets in gold.

The London market opens while Zurich is still trading. It quite often takes its starting cue from Zurich. So goes gold around the world each day.

L is for London, New York, Hong Kong, Zurich—The sun never sets on the gold market.

Chapter 13

M is for . . .
Myths and Realities about Gold

Gold has its critics. Yet most of their criticism is ill-founded and amounts to little more than good propaganda for those who fear strong gold demand will divert investor interest from the equities markets and the dollar. You have probably heard or read most of the standard criticisms.

Here are concise and complete rebuttals—the last words on the merits of gold.

Myth: Gold is not a good portfolio item because it doesn't pay interest.

Reality: The fact that gold does not pay interest is its greatest strength. If gold were to pay interest, the return on your gold would be dependent on the performance of another individual or institution. This, of course, is the case with paper assets such as bonds, bank-certified deposits, money-market accounts, and even stocks. The contractual relationship between the creditor and the debtor can be a paper asset's greatest strength. It can also be its greatest weakness. An additional and often complicating factor is that paper assets are directly affected by the performance of the currency in which they are denominated.

Gold, on the other hand, does not suffer such ambiguity. It is a stand-alone investment independent of government largesse or the performance of another individual or institution. This is gold's greatest strength. Even though gold does not pay interest directly, it is interesting to note that over any extended period of time the interest rate of the currency becomes imputed in the price. Gold historically seeks a price level that takes into account the inflation rate of currency. This compensates for its non-interest-bearing status.

Myth: In the long run, stocks always outperform gold; therefore, there's no reason to own gold.

Reality: This might be the greatest gold myth of them all. From 1970 to 2010, stocks have risen 1509% and gold, 4374%. Gold outperformed stocks over the period by nearly three times. From 2008 to 2010, when the stock market was widely touted as still a good place to invest even amid the financial crisis, gold still outperformed the Dow Jones Industrial Average—a 30% increase for gold to a 15% increase for stocks.

Myth: Gold is just another commodity, like pork bellies.

Reality: Gold trades on the commodities exchanges along with pork bellies and other commodities, but there the similarity ends. Unlike other commodities, which are produced primarily for consumption, gold alone is accumulated and saved. It is also the only commodity used as money to facilitate future consumption. Most of the gold ever produced still exists today in one form or another. You cannot say the same thing about pork bellies, soybeans, or sugar. The gold you might someday purchase could very well have been part of the treasury of Rome, or used by Marco Polo in his first visit to China, or circulated as currency in the Old West. This money function separates it from the commodity complex and gives it a special place at the very top of the value scale. Those who relegate gold to the status of "just another commodity" usually do so because they either fear gold or do not like competing against it. By denigrating it, they hope to subdue public accumulation—an exercise in futility. Gold is the enduring commodity.

Myth: Gold is a barbarous relic of past monetary systems, irrelevant in today's fast-moving, computerized markets.

Reality: Gold is held as a reserve asset in nearly every central bank in the world. It serves as an asset of last resort to be used for grave international crises such as war, economic calamity, environmental and weather disasters, and the like. Former U.S. Federal Reserve Chairman Paul Volcker made these comments about gold and central banking in answer to the barbarous relic claim:

> "We sometimes forget that central banking as we know it today is, in fact, largely an invention of the past hundred years or so, even though a few central banks can trace their ancestry back to the early nineteenth century or before. It is a sobering fact that the prominence of central banks in this century has coincided with a general tendency toward more inflation, not less. By and large, if the overriding objective is price stability, we did better with the nineteenth century gold standard and passive central banks, with currency boards, or even with 'free banking.' The truly unique power of a central bank, after all, is the power to create money, and ultimately the power to create is the power to destroy."

Other central bankers, including former U.S. Federal Reserve Chairman Alan Greenspan, have voiced similar admiration for this barbarous relic. Gold today has the same relevance it has always enjoyed. It is the asset of last resort and has universal value for both individual investors and nation-states.

Myth: World governments in conjunction with the central banks control the gold price. They intend to hold that price down.

Reality: In each instance in modern monetary history, when governments and central banks (including the U.S. federal government) acted to hold the gold price down, the price was on the verge of moving substantially higher due to the inflationary policies these very same institutions were encouraging. Their activities to hold gold down amounted to exercises in futility, only delaying the dominant, underlying trend. Far from being able to control gold, to the consternation of some central bankers and governments, they, too, must answer ultimately to what the gold market is telling them. When it comes to currency value, gold is the master of all and the slave of none.

Myth: Gold is in a bubble like the tech-stock and real estate bubbles, and as a result, should be avoided as an investment.

Reality: The claim that gold is in a bubble brings to mind the story of Saudi Arabia's King Ibn Saud and his sale of oil concessions to the major oil companies in 1933. As payment he received 35,000 British Sovereigns—a coin many of you hold in your own sovereign wealth funds. The good king understood the difference between the value of gold and the value of a paper promise. At the time, British Sovereigns were valued at $8.24 each, or $288,365 for the 35,000-coin lot. The price of oil in 1933 was about 85 cents a barrel. A British Sovereign, as a result, could buy about ten barrels of oil. Today those same Sovereigns would bring a little less than $12 million at melt value ($411.00 each/$1750 per ounce gold price) and a barrel of oil is selling for about $117.00. Thus, a British Sovereign can buy about three and a half barrels of oil—a statistic that gives you an inkling of gold's current under-valuation. *For gold to buy the same amount of oil now that it did in 1933, the price would have to go to nearly $5000 per ounce—an interesting calculation for those who say gold is in a bubble.*

Myth: Gold is a speculative, volatile investment that should be avoided by conservative investors.

Reality: It is not gold that changes in value but currencies. What you could purchase with an ounce of gold a hundred years ago, you can purchase with an ounce of gold today. The reason for the spikes dominating the gold charts over the long cycle is not gold's volatility, but rather government and/or central bank intervention to suppress the price. Once market forces overcame the intervention, gold sought its natural price level, which often proved to be multiples of the interventionists' target range. Hence the spikes. If the interventionists had not acted to keep the price of gold down, the chart would have a more gradual rise, and gold's critics would be unable to make claims about its volatility.

Myth: Gold is an unpatriotic investment.

Reality: It has become a small world. Investors now invest their money in economies all over the world. Is it unpatriotic for an investor to buy Swiss annuities, or a Japanese equities fund, or a South African gold fund? Would these choices be considered un-American? Probably not. More likely, they would be considered prudent diversifications. There is also the question of whether citizens are obligated to lose their hard-earned wealth holding a currency that is being systematically debased by misguided monetary authorities.

Far from being unpatriotic, citizens who accumulate gold may be the exact opposite. These citizens could very well turn out to be the country's most farsighted, devoted, and patriotic resource. In China and Japan, where the buildup of dollar reserves threatens the nation's long-term economic stability, the government encourages citizens to own gold, and gold imports, as a result, have grown rapidly.

Indeed, the fact that certain citizens have the wisdom to accumulate gold may someday be this country's saving grace. If the dollar were to fail, the gold accumulated in the United States by American citizens would become part of the capital base required for this nation to recover—a thought worth pondering as we close this section.

M is for Myths and Realities about Gold—Now you know the rest of the story.

Chapter 14

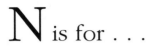N is for . . .

Navigating Uncharted Waters: Which Investments Performed Best in the Tumultuous "Oh-Oh" Decade?

"The next Fourth Turning is due to begin shortly after the new millennium, midway through the oh-oh decade. Around the year 2005, a sudden spark will catalyze a Crisis mood. Remnants of the old social order will disintegrate. Political and economic trust will implode. Real hardship will beset the land, with severe distress that could involve questions of class, race, nation, and empire."
—William Strauss and Neil Howe,
The Fourth Turning, 1997

The first decade of the twenty-first century was among the most tumultuous in American financial history. This chapter reviews how various investment vehicles performed under the stressful social and economic circumstances predicted for that time period by William Strauss and Neil Howe in *The Fourth Turning*. If Strauss and Howe are correct that we have entered a new era, as described above, then it might be useful to review how various investments performed during its initial stages.

The "Oh-Oh" decade, as Strauss and Howe called it, lived up to its name:

- The Y2K Scare (2000)
- The dot.com stock bubble (2000)

- Enron, Tyco, and Worldcom collapses (2001)
- The terrorist attack on World Trade Center and Pentagon (2001)
- The second war in Iraq (2003)
- Hurricane Katrina and its aftermath (2005)
- The housing bubble crash (2006)
- The Wall Street financial crisis and bailouts (2008)
- The stock market meltdown (2008–2009)
- The sovereign debt crisis in Europe (2009–2012)

A popular lyric by songwriter Ray LaMontagne seemed to capture the mind-set of the nation: "Trouble, trouble, trouble, trouble...Feels like every time I get back on my feet, she come around and knock me down again..." The bard was saved, as one might expect, by the love of a woman, but one wonders who or what is going to save the world economy.

Over the last decade, the middle class has seen its savings dwindle against an ever-rising cost of living. The once vaunted pension plan that was supposed to take the baby boomers to a happy and secure retirement was "cut to the quick" by a stagnant and volatile stock market. All the while, 0% interest rates nearly eliminated returns on savings instruments. In the months following the Lehman Brothers collapse in 2008, it became clear that an individual with a million dollars in the bank could not afford to retire. With yields so low, a retiree could not pay his or her expenses without dipping into the principal.

Overall, the 2000s unfolded as a disinflationary period characterized by a declining inflation rate, rising unemployment, and stagnant to declining investment markets. Gold rose steadily throughout the disinflationary 2000s, as you are about to see, putting to rest the long-held notion that it is strictly an inflation hedge.

Stocks, using the Dow Jones Industrial Average as a measure, did not fare well over the "Oh-Oh" decade,

The ABCs of Gold Investing

Figure 19. Comparative Investment Survey Table (1999–2009)

	Gold	Silver	DJIA	Gold Stocks	Median Home	Commodities	CPI	$ Index
1999	290.00	5.33	11,497.00	67.72	164,800.00	196.27	174.00	101.58
2005	513.00	8.83	10,507.00	128.03	238,600.00	438.36	196.80	83.71
2007	834.00	14.76	13,264.00	173.32	227,700.00	592.20	210.00	77.84
2008	870.00	10.79	8,776.00	123.85	229,600.00	345.50	210.00	74.34
2009	1087.00	17.00	10,428.00	168.25	222,600.00	481.75	215.90	77.75
10-year	275%	219%	-9%	148%	35%	146%	24%	-24%

Sources: All data year end. Gold/Silver, London Fix; DJIA/Dow Jones Industrial Average; Gold Stocks/XAU Index; Median Home, Census Bureau; Commodities/Goldman Sachs Commodity Index; CPI/Consumer Price Index Bureau Labor Statistics; $ Index/U.S. Dollar Index

112

Figure 20. **Comparative Investment Survey Chart (2000–2009)**

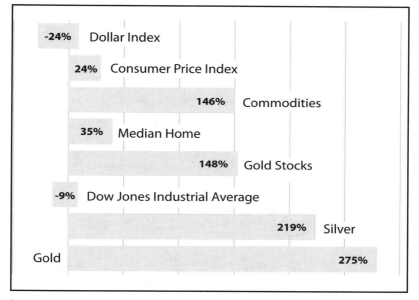

losing an average of just over 9% of their value overall, and nearly 34% during the two years (2007 and 2008) encompassing the financial crisis. Gold stocks, due to their exposure to the gold's price appreciation, rose 148% over the ten-year period, but cratered with the rest of the stock market in 2008. Through it all, the dollar has been in a protracted bear market, falling over 24% against a basket of currencies over the "Oh-Oh" decade.

All things considered, the value of the median family home fared fairly well following the credit crisis, falling only 7%. It was the underlying mortgage securities that became a problem as the crisis progressed, and highly overvalued residential real estate in select areas.

Throughout the decade, silver kept up with gold for the most part, but dropped precipitously from year-end 2007 to year-end 2008—shedding nearly 40% of its value. Gold initially took a hit in 2008 but was also the first major asset to recover, ending the year very close to where it began. Its resilient performance demonstrated the public's allegiance to gold as the ultimate asset of last resort and disaster hedge.

Gold shined like a beacon through the tumultuous "Oh-Oh" decade, appreciating a total of 275%. Even during the stressful times of 2007–2009, gold still managed a 30% gain at a time when commodities overall *fell* nearly 19%—a circumstance that flies in the face of the criticism that it is simply another commodity. Similarly, gold outperformed the consumer price index by a wide margin, thereby buttressing its reputation as an effective inflation hedge. If the "Oh-Oh" decade was a test, then stocks, the dollar, and interest-bearing accounts (not shown) failed miserably; silver, commodities, and gold stocks passed with flying colors; and gold was asked to prepare the valedictory address.

N is for Navigating Uncharted Waters—Get a sturdy ship and a stout sail; keep an eye on the horizon.

Chapter 15

O is for . . .
Own the Gold; Make the Rules

Put ten ounces of gold in someone's hand and you will see an immediate smile of recognition; and anyone who has held ten ounces of gold in his or her hand understands what that smile of recognition is all about. The weight and feel of real gold delivers an instantaneous message of the solidity, value, and monetary function of gold.

There is an old adage: "He who owns the gold makes the rules." No one is quite sure where that saying originated, but it has been around as long as I have been involved in the gold market. It is often referred to as the "golden rule." Originally, the saying associated wealth with power and was usually delivered with a shrug. Then it came to be associated with owning something of enduring value as opposed to a fiat currency that was subject to debasement.

In contemporary times, it has taken on a whole new meaning, one meant to differentiate the ownership of the metal itself from so-called "paper gold" alternatives, or derivatives—gold stocks, futures, options, leverage accounts, and exchange traded funds (ETFs). Though each of these paper options can play a positive role in the overall investment portfolio, none is a substitute for owning gold in its physical form—coins and bullion.

Gold Stocks

Gold stocks are stocks first and gold second. This is an important distinction for investors to make. I have talked directly with hundreds of gold owners over the years and I cannot recall a single one saying something like "I think the economy is in trouble, I am going to buy some gold stocks." Gold stocks carry the same inherent risks found in other stocks, and few would view either as a safe-haven store of value. As a matter of fact, in the last four stock market crashes—1929, 1935, 1987, and 2008—gold stocks tumbled with the rest of the market. Overall, from 2002 to 2011, gold stocks performed well, but they did not keep up with bullion. Using the Philadelphia Gold and Silver Index (XAU) as a benchmark, gold stocks during that period rose 167% while gold bullion rose 450%.

You could presumably own a gold stock during a period of rising gold prices and not participate in the uptrend simply because a company had diminishing prospects in the eyes of the investment community. This is precisely what happened to a good many shareholders during the early years of gold's price run-up. A number of large mining companies were excluded from gold's bull market because they had hedged their production by selling their gold forward for future delivery. As it turned out, they sold too early at a discount and sometimes a severe discount to the rising market price. Nationalization, labor disputes, and environmental protection measures are ever-present risks to mining companies above and beyond the everyday risks of operating a complicated industrial concern.

On the positive side of the ledger, a well-run gold mining company could greatly benefit from demand growth from private investors and institutions, but especially from central banks, should the trend toward diversification of reserves continue into the second decade of the twenty-first century. Needless to say, any attempt to benefit from the trend would be predicated on solid reserves and sound management practices. Analyzing the viability of a publicly traded mining company is a tricky business, and the best bet for most investors is go with a mutual fund or broker who understands this highly specialized field.

Gold Exchange Traded Funds (ETFs)

Gold ETFs are more a vehicle for speculation on the price than ownership of the metal for safe-haven purposes. Essentially, an ETF issues shares that represent a weight of bullion. These shares are then traded on the market like any stock. In the case of the SPDR Gold Trust, the largest gold ETF, each share represents one-tenth of an ounce of gold. These instruments give the impression of metal ownership, but in most cases, the owner of ETF shares cannot redeem those shares for the physical metal, unless one is willing to take the minimum delivery—a 400-ounce bar—perhaps the most illiquid gold bullion item. Another weakness in ETFs is that to pay storage and insurance fees, a small amount of metal is liquidated annually. As such, the amount of metal represented by each share diminishes over time.

An additional disadvantage to ETF ownership, and one often overlooked even by investment professionals, is the fact that its shares, like any publicly traded shares, can be sold short. Tim Hatton, author of *The New Fiduciary Standard*, a book that outlines prudent practices for investment professionals, described the concern as follows: "[T]he biggest cause for concern is due to the ability to short shares, which is not found in the prospectus. When you purchase shares in GLD (The SPDR Gold Trust) those shares represent a fractional and undivided interest in the trust, which is your share of physical gold. When shares are shorted, an additional fractional and undivided interest is created but no additional gold is purchased. Suddenly someone else may have a claim on your share of gold."

He goes on to say, "I do view all of these negative possibilities as remote and it is hard to compete with the liquidity of GLD in financial markets that are performing routinely. However, the reason to own gold is to have an asset that will perform well in extremely unfavorable economic times. There is no doubt in my mind that physical possession is the preferred way to hold gold simply because fewer things outside of your control can go wrong."

In 2005, ETF gold demand, according to the World Gold Council, was 208 tonnes. In 2009, ETF off-take was a record 617 tonnes, but by 2011 the volume dropped to 154 tonnes. Gold coin and bullion demand, by contrast, over that same period roughly doubled from 776 tonnes to 1487 tonnes. Note, too, that sales in gold coins and bullion outpaced the ETFs in 2011 by a factor of nearly ten to one. ETFs have been a favorite with hedge funds and financial institutions, but at the same time there has been significant movement within this group to actual bullion ownership stored in depositories around the world. When the University of Texas Investment Management Company, which oversees an endowment fund for the University of Texas and Texas A&M, decided in 2011 to purchase $1 billion in gold, it opted to take ownership of bullion bars delivered to its account at a New York depository.

Gold Futures, Options, and Other Leveraged Accounts

Futures, options, and leveraged accounts are among the riskiest capital allocations an investor can make and no less so with gold and the other precious metals. In the case of futures contracts, leverage plays an important role, as you can purchase a gold contract of 100 troy ounces, for example, with a margin requirement of roughly 5%— or twenty-to-one leverage. If the market moves up 5% you theoretically double your money (before costs). If it goes down 5%, you lose your margin and need to pay into the account or you lose the position. As for leveraged (loan) accounts, generally offered outside the purview of the Commodities Futures Trading Commission, you can purchase a precious metals product in the form of coins or bars and then take out a loan that usually amounts to 80% of value at the time of the purchase—or a leverage of five to one.

Though disclosure is usually made at the time of the purchase, investors are often surprised to discover the loss of the entirety of their principal if the market moves sufficiently against the position. In other words, precious metals leverage accounts are just as risky as investments in the futures' market. In addition, accrued interest is usually added to the loan as are commissions, spread, and storage costs, all of which add to the amount of appreciation required to show a profit.

Options—puts and calls (shorts and longs)—can expire either at a premium over what the buyer paid, or they can expire worthless. It has been said that 85% of all options' positions expire worthless. Complicating matters, options contracts have a time limit and the investment must go up or down sufficiently to produce a profit within that time frame. Options are written against existing commodities contracts traded on an exchange, or they can be negotiated by private contract in the London forward market. Leveraged accounts of any kind—futures, options, or loan accounts—are very risky propositions and are the polar opposite of fully owned physical metal positions.

If you see yourself primarily as a saver, as opposed to a speculative investor, it is important to meet your physical ownership objectives before moving into the riskier arenas briefly covered here. Too often, the gold saver is diverted from his or her true objectives by the lure of speculative profit. A strategy of speculating in gold derivatives, for example, with the intention of generating profits that can then be converted to gold coins or bullion rarely works. The other side of the speculative equation—losses—more often than not takes the wind out of the investor's sails.

Please be advised that none of the foregoing is meant to be investment advice, but simply an overview so that you can compare and assess the risks associated with these types of investments against outright gold ownership.

O is for Own the gold; make the rules—Don't confuse a speculative paper investment with owning the real thing.

Chapter 16

P is for . . .
Post-1971 History of Gold

History is philosophy learned from examples.
—Thucydides

Mark Twain once said that "history does not repeat, it rhymes." For the student of financial markets, gold's history offers a prism through which one can gain a more thorough understanding of the contemporary economy. It also lays the groundwork for the investor hoping to make an educated guess as to how the past might very well rhyme with the future.

The most significant events in the modern history of gold are the Gold Standard Act of 1900, by which the United States joined most of Europe in a gold-based economic system; the Federal Reserve Act of 1913, by which the United States entered on the long road to severing the dollar's link to gold; Franklin Delano Roosevelt's devaluation of the dollar in the 1930s and the subsequent call-in of gold; the Bretton Woods Agreement following World War II, which fixed the dollar to gold and the rest of the world's currencies to the dollar; and finally the abandonment of Bretton Woods and the further devaluation of the dollar during Richard Nixon's presidency in the early 1970s.

Modern Economic Era

For our purposes, the modern economic era began in 1971. That year, President Richard Nixon abandoned the Bretton Woods Agreement, devalued the dollar, raised the fixed price of gold to $37.50, and closed the gold window to stop an international run on the U.S. gold reserve. Previous to Nixon's actions, the United States had reduced its once prodigious gold hoard of over 20,000 tonnes to just a little over 8000 tonnes in an effort to support the $35.00 international benchmark. Much of the U.S. hoard went overseas, particularly to Europe. Two years later, the U.S. government raised its fixed gold price to $42.22. The dollar was freed to float against the rest of the world's currencies. Gold began to trade freely in gold markets around the world. Nixon's actions also gave a green light to uninhibited budget and trade deficits. The United States was no longer required to deliver gold to any nation that stepped up to the gold window and demanded gold for dollars.

In subsequent years, the severance of the relationship between gold and the dollar would become a license to inflate. To this day, the U.S. gold reserve of roughly 260 million ounces ostensibly is valued at $42.22 per ounce, despite the fact that the free market price is closer to thirty or forty times that number. At the time, Richard Nixon proclaimed, "We are all Keynesians." This was his way of saying that the forces of sound money were no longer to be represented in American politics, not even by the hard money and conservatively inclined Republican Party. The abrogation of the Bretton Woods Agreement—the international economic structure based on gold that had been in place since World War II—laid the foundation for the modern private gold market.

When politicians took gold out of the national money, which is what Nixon did, the need for private gold ownership was enhanced as a means to protect wealth. By 1973, gold climbed to $120 as price inflation gripped the nation. In that year, the federal debt stood at $466 billion, small by today's standards and representing only 34% of the gross domestic product. Double-digit inflation hit the American economy in 1974. The stock market corrected significantly. That year Richard Nixon resigned from office under the pall of the Watergate scandal. The gold price hit $200, 5.5 times the price targeted in the late 1960s as gold's benchmark.

1975–1979: Transition to Final Stage
of Gold's Bull Market

The recession years of 1975 and 1976 saw gold in a downtrend, bottoming out at $104. Jimmy Carter was elected president. Continued loose monetary policies, deficit spending, and an embargo against the United States by the Organization of Petroleum Exporting Countries (OPEC) exacerbated an already fragile international monetary situation. Inflation dominated the financial scene. The International Monetary Fund (IMF) and the United States launched monthly gold auctions in 1975. Publicly, the government announced that the sales were intended to meet the newly generated demand resulting from the legalization of private gold ownership in the United States. The real reasons for the sales were to demonetize gold once and for all and to keep the price below $150. The IMF and the U.S. Treasury sold nearly 1200 tonnes of metal—to no avail. By 1977, the price broke out again. In 1978, it was trading in the $250 range. After sales were curtailed in 1978, gold, with the impediment to its upward climb removed, went through the roof, making progress toward its then all-time high. By 1979, the nation and the world had become engulfed in a full-blown monetary crisis. In January 1980, gold peaked at $875 in a buying frenzy.

1980–1987: Recession Years,
Then a Recovery and a Quiet Gold Market

Ronald Reagan, vowing to bring stability to a troubled nation, was elected president in 1980, unseating the incumbent Jimmy Carter. Interest rates hit 19%, an unheard-of level, but this cooled the gold market and brought some stability to the dollar. Gold prices bottomed at just under $300 in 1982; but in 1983, in what turned out to be a minor currency crisis in Europe resulting from the stronger dollar, gold investment demand drove the price back up to $500. Also in 1983, the United States posted its highest unemployment rate since 1941.

The American economy had entered an era of high interest rates, high unemployment, and a subdued, yet still high inflation rate. These circumstances dominated the financial markets as well, and the groundwork was laid for the long-term bull market in stocks and the dollar. A combination of high real interest rates (yields minus the inflation rate), inexpensive imports, and an abundance of oil kept the inflation rate in check and the gold price from rising radically.

The national debt went over $2 trillion, a disturbing benchmark at the time. Seventy banks failed in 1987 alone, the most since the Great Depression, and the United States became the greatest debtor nation on earth. In October 1987 the stock market crashed, and gold shot back up to $500.

1988–1992: Another Recession, the S&L Crisis, Gold Remains Subdued

George H.W. Bush became president in 1988 and was immediately greeted by the worst banking crisis in U.S. history. In what came to be known as the S&L crisis, $300 billion was committed to bailing out mismanaged and sometimes fraudulently run savings-and-loan institutions. The national debt went over the $3 trillion mark, just three years after breaking the $2 trillion figure. By 1990, the economy was again in recession. For the first time since 1980, the United States posted a negative growth number for the gross domestic product. The Soviet Union broke up, forever altering the international political landscape. East and West Germany reunified as a single nation-state.

The United States subdued Saddam Hussein and Iraq in the (first) Gulf War, the highlight of George H.W. Bush's

124

presidency. The Cold War ended. In the United States, massive back-to-back deficits pushed the accumulated federal debt over $4 trillion, just two years after breaking the $3 trillion mark. In 1992, the United States ran its biggest deficit in history—$290 billion. Gold remained in the doldrums under the influence of persistent official sales and forward selling from the mining companies. Throughout this period gold remained subdued trading in a narrow range between $330 and $425 per ounce.

1993–1997: Mexico and Pacific Rim Crises, DJIA Hits Record

Gold traded at $330 per ounce level as Bill Clinton was inaugurated president in 1993. Pushed by a Japanese banking crisis, a monetary crisis in Europe, and the belief that the Clinton administration would rekindle an inflationary economy, resurgent gold demand drove the price back to the $425 level. Gold production began to fall, while demand reached record levels worldwide, particularly in the Far East. Only record forward sales by the mines and official central bank sales (detailed in chapter 6) kept the price from bolting higher. In 1995, the United States, mired in economic problems of its own, bailed out Mexico.

The federal government shut down during a budget battle between the Republican-controlled U.S. Congress and the Democratic Clinton administration. Gold began to rise in early 1996, once again challenging the $425 mark. The national debt went past $5 trillion, a figure representing over 70% of the gross domestic product. As 1996 drew to a close, gold returned to the $370 level under pressure from heavy forward sales by South African mining companies. Alan Greenspan warned of "irrational exuberance" in the financial markets.

Early 1997 saw the Dow Jones Industrial Average (DJIA) reach a record high. The gold price remained relatively flat for most of the year, held down by central bank sales from the Netherlands, Australia, and Argentina. A study group in Switzerland recommended a phased sale of 1400 tonnes from the Swiss national reserve. An Asian currency crisis took hold and spread from nation to nation in the Pacific Rim, wreaking havoc in one economy after another. By the end of the year, the Dow had begun to fall rapidly, signaling the end of the long bull market in stocks and vindicating Alan Greenspan's earlier warning about an "irrational exuberance" gripping the nation.

1998–1999: Long-Term
Gold Bear Market Shows Signs of Ending

The year 1998 began with concerns mounting globally that a financial crisis in the Pacific Rim that later came to be known as the Asian Contagion might not be contained. Russia defaulted on its national debt, wreaking havoc with financial institutions globally. Long Term Capital Management, a hedge fund advised by a Nobel Prize laureate, collapsed and was bailed out by key Wall Street financial firms. Amid all the uncertainty, gold hit a nineteen-year low of $270. Concerned that the Asian Contagion could affect the banking system in the industrialized world, private investment demand put strong pressure on available gold supplies.

Although the year started quietly, 1999 turned out to be one of the most important and volatile years for gold since the early 1980s. In May, the Bank of England announced it would sell over half of its remaining gold reserve by auction. The gold market went into a tailspin, ratcheting down to $250. Then, in September 1999, the market abruptly moved to nearly $340 per ounce when the fifteen top European central banks agreed formally to cap gold sales and leasing. That announcement pushed a number of hedged mining companies into financial straits, including Ghana's Ashanti Goldfields and Canada's Cambior Mines. The euro was officially introduced.

The year 1999 is generally believed to be a transitional period for gold—the last year of a long secular *bear*

126

market and the beginning of what became a long-term secular *bull* market. Safe-haven, hedging risks associated with the year 2000 (Y2K) computer scare and the spread of the Asian Contagion to U.S.-based banks, gold buyers pushed premiums on historic U.S., and European gold coins to double previous levels.

2000–2003: Gold Begins Long Rise

In 2000, the stock market's woes continued and investors increasingly began looking around for alternatives, with gold becoming one of the chief beneficiaries. The Dow Jones Industrial Average (DJIA) peaked at over 11,700. On September 11, 2001, hijackers crashed jetliners into the World Trade Center, the Pentagon, and a Pennsylvania field, setting off a new wave of gold buying among international investors concerned about the potential for a long-term war against terrorism and the effect it might have on the flow of oil from the Middle East.

Later in 2001, gold returned to a low of $250 and thereafter began a rally that took it back over the $400 level for the first time since 1993. In both 2002 and 2003, gold appreciated in the 20% range. Hedge fund and producer buying underpinned the gold market action as scandals involving several major investment houses besieged Wall Street. In 2001, the United States launched a war in Afghanistan, and the Second Iraq War was launched in 2003. The United States ran record trade and budget deficits.

2004–2011: Gold Breaks Out,
Financial Crisis Spreads Globally

In 2004, the International Monetary Fund warned that America's twin deficits (trade balance and budget deficit) threatened the world economy. Switzerland announced its sale of 250 tonnes of gold. China emerged as a growing economic powerhouse with a great deal of speculation about its gold demand. The world economy fully rebounded from the 2001–2002 recession and the

Federal Reserve raised interest rates five times in a twelve-month period. The first gold exchange traded fund was launched largely as a vehicle for mutual funds, hedge funds, and pension funds to participate in the gold market. It was greeted with enthusiasm by both the funds and the general public. In 2006 gold broke over the $600 mark and traded in a range between $600 and $700 well into 2007, hitting twenty-five-year highs.

By the end of 2007 gold surpassed the $800 mark as the dollar hit new lows against the euro. The first signs of the subprime credit crisis emerged. Central banks globally injected trillions into the financial system to combat the crisis. The commodities complex rose to thirty-two-year highs. The German Bundesbank, amid speculation that it might sell some of its large gold reserve, announced it would not be a seller. In succession, Germany's Sachsen Landesbank nearly collapsed; the United Kingdom's Northern Rock Bank experienced a bank run; and in late 2008, the U.S. insurance/banking giants Bear Stearns, AIG, and Lehman Brothers all collapsed. Bear Stearns and AIG were bailed out, but Lehman Brothers was not, thus touching off a general financial panic in the United States with global implications. In addition, Fannie Mae and Freddie Mac, the quasi-government housing authorities that purchase mortgages from private lenders, were nationalized by the U.S. federal government.

Global demand for gold as a safe haven rose to record levels and the price jumped over the $900 per ounce level in 2008 and the $1100 level in 2009. China announced significant additions to its national gold reserve as a hedge against its massive dollar holdings. By late 2009, speculation about sovereign debt problems in Greece, Spain, and Portugal began to trouble world markets. Concern continued about U.S. trade and fiscal deficits. The U.S. national debt approached $13 trillion with nearly $2 trillion added to the debt in 2009 alone—a record that surpassed the highest previous addition by

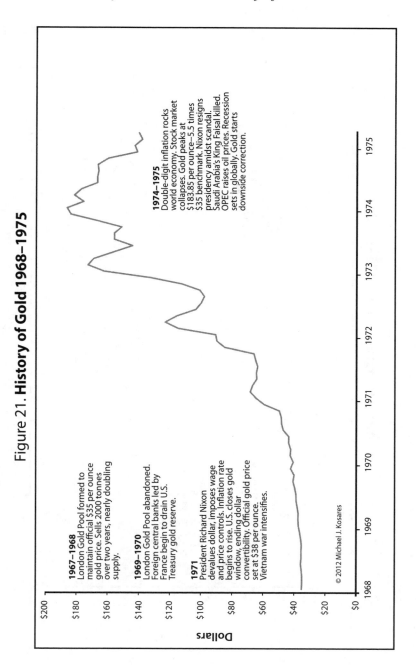

Figure 21. **History of Gold 1968–1975**

1967–1968
London Gold Pool formed to maintain official $35 per ounce gold price. Sells 2000 tonnes over two years, nearly doubling supply.

1969–1970
London Gold Pool abandoned. Foreign central banks led by France begin to drain U.S. Treasury gold reserve.

1971
President Richard Nixon devalues dollar, imposes wage and price controls. Inflation rate begins to rise. U.S. closes gold window, ending dollar convertibility. Official gold price set at $38 per ounce. Vietnam war intensifies.

1974–1975
Double-digit inflation rocks world economy. Stock market collapses. Gold peaks at $183.85 per ounce—5.5 times $35 benchmark. Nixon resigns presidency amidst scandal. Saudi Arabia's King Faisal killed. OPEC raises oil prices. Recession sets in globally. Gold starts downside correction.

© 2012 Michael J. Kosares

Figure 22. **History of Gold 1976–1983**

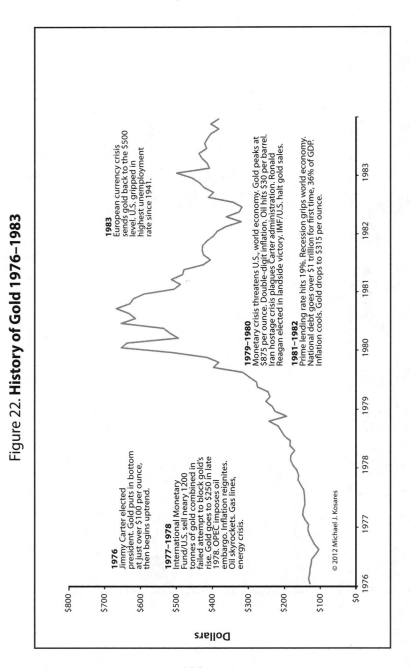

1976
Jimmy Carter elected president. Gold puts in bottom at just over $100 per ounce, then begins uptrend.

1977–1978
International Monetary Fund/U.S. sell nearly 1200 tonnes of gold combined in failed attempt to block gold's rise. Gold goes to $250 in late 1978. OPEC imposes oil embargo. Inflation reignites. Oil skyrockets. Gas lines, energy crisis.

1979–1980
Monetary crisis threatens U.S., world economy. Gold peaks at $875 per ounce. Double-digit inflation. Oil hits $30 per barrel. Iran hostage crisis plagues Carter administration. Ronald Reagan elected in landslide victory. IMF/U.S. halt gold sales.

1981–1982
Prime lending rate hits 19%. Recession grips world economy. National debt goes over $1 trillion for first time, 36% of GDP. Inflation cools. Gold drops to $315 per ounce.

1983
European currency crisis sends gold back to the $500 level. U.S. gripped in highest unemployment rate since 1941.

© 2012 Michael J. Kosares

Dollars

Figure 23. **History of Gold 1984–1991**

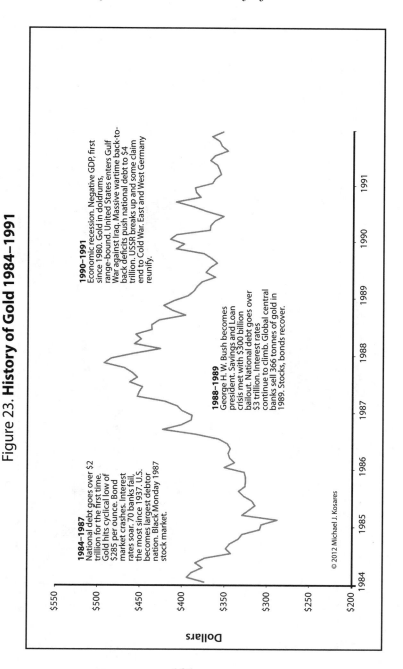

1984–1987
National debt goes over $2 trillion for the first time. Gold hits cyclical low of $285 per ounce. Bond market crashes. Interest rates soar. 70 banks fail, the most since 1937. U.S. becomes largest debtor nation. Black Monday 1987 stock market.

1988–1989
George H. W. Bush becomes president. Savings and Loan crisis met with $300 billion bailout. National debt goes over $3 trillion. Interest rates continue to climb. Global central banks sell 366 tonnes of gold in 1989. Stocks, bonds recover.

1990–1991
Economic recession. Negative GDP, first since 1980. Gold in doldrums, range-bound. United States enters Gulf War against Iraq. Massive wartime back-to-back deficits push national debt to $4 trillion. USSR breaks up and some claim end to Cold War. East and West Germany reunify.

131

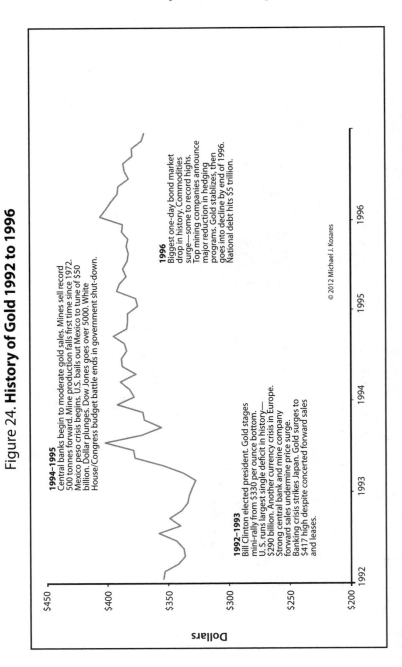

Figure 24. **History of Gold 1992 to 1996**

1994-1995
Central banks begin to moderate gold sales. Mines sell record 500 tonnes forward. Mine production falls first time since 1972. Mexico peso crisis begins. U.S. bails out Mexico to tune of $50 billion. Dollar plunges. Dow Jones goes over 5000. White House/Congress budget battle ends in government shut-down.

1996
Biggest one-day bond market drop in history. Commodities surge—some to record highs. Top mining companies announce major reduction in hedging programs. Gold stabilizes, then goes into decline by end of 1996. National debt hits $5 trillion.

1992-1993
Bill Clinton elected president. Gold stages mini-rally from $330 per ounce bottom. U.S. runs largest single deficit in history—$290 billion. Another currency crisis in Europe. Strong central bank and mine company forward sales undermine price surge. Banking crisis strikes Japan. Gold surges to $417 high despite concerted forward sales and leases.

© 2012 Michael J. Kosares

Dollars

$450 $400 $350 $300 $250 $200

1992 1993 1994 1995 1996

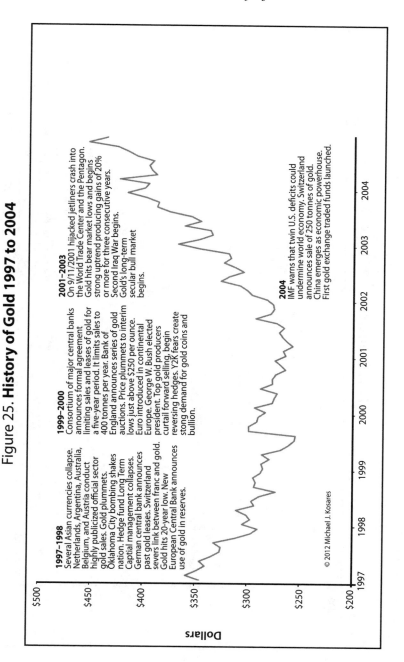

Figure 25. **History of Gold 1997 to 2004**

1997-1998
Several Asian currencies collapse. Netherlands, Argentina, Australia, Belgium, and Austria conduct highly publicized official sector gold sales. Gold plummets. Oklahoma City bombing shakes nation. Hedge fund Long Term Captial management collapses. German central bank announces past gold leases. Switzerland severs link between franc and gold. Gold hits 20-year low. New European Central Bank announces use of gold in reserves.

1999-2000
Consortium of major central banks announces formal agreement limiting sales and leases of gold for a five-year period. It limits sales to 400 tonnes per year. Bank of England announces series of gold auctions. Price plummets to interim lows just above $250 per ounce. Euro introduced in continental Europe. George W. Bush elected president. Top gold producers curtail forward selling, begin reversing hedges. Y2K fears create stong demand for gold coins and bullion.

2001-2003
On 9/11/2001 hijacked jetliners crash into the World Trade Center and the Pentagon. Gold hits bear market lows and begins strong uptrend producing gains of 20% or more for three consecutive years. Second Iraq War begins. Gold's long-term secular bull market begins.

2004
IMF warns that twin U.S. deficits could undermine world economy. Switzerland announces sale of 250 tonnes of gold. China emerges as economic powerhouse. First gold exchange traded funds launched.

© 2012 Michael J. Kosares

Figure 26. **History of Gold 2005 to 2011**

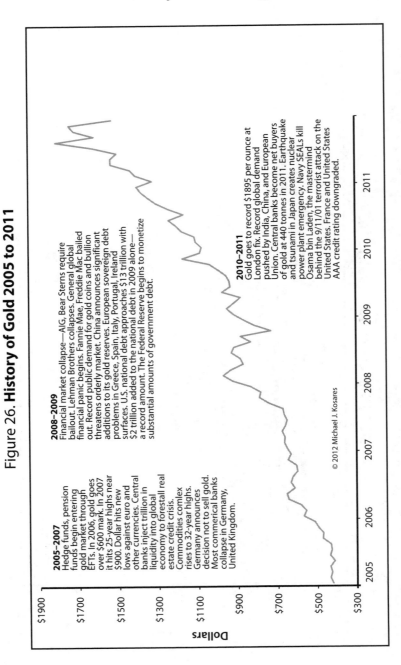

2005–2007
Hedge funds, pension funds begin entering gold market through EFTs. In 2006, gold goes over $600 mark. In 2007 it hits 25-year highs near $900. Dollar hits new lows against euro and other currencies. Central banks inject trillion in liquidity into global economy to forestall real estate credit crisis. Commodities comlex rises to 32-year highs. Germany announces decision not to sell gold. Most commerical banks collapse in Germany, United Kingdom.

2008–2009
Financial market collapse—AIG, Bear Sterns require bailout. Lehman Brothers collapses. General global financial panic begins. Fannie Mae, Freddie Mac bailed out. Record public demand for gold coins and bullion threatens orderly market. China announces significant additions to its gold reserves. European sovereign debt problems in Greece, Spain, Italy, Portugal, Ireland surfaces. U.S. national debt approaches $13 trillion with $2 trillion added to the national debt in 2009 alone—a record amount. The Federal Reserve begins to monetize substantial amounts of government debt.

2010–2011
Gold goes to record $1895 per ounce at London fix. Record global demand pushed by India, China, and European Union. Central banks become net buyers of gold at 440 tonnes in 2011. Earthquake and tsunami in Japan creates nuclear power plant emergency. Navy SEALs kill Osama bin Laden, the mastermind behind the 9/11 terrorist attack on the United States. France and United States AAA credit rating downgraded.

© 2012 Michael J. Kosares

134

nearly four times. The national debt to GDP ratio hovered at nearly 100%. In 1971, the year this history begins, that same ratio was 35%.

In 2010, global demand for gold again registered a record with China, India, and the European Union leading the way. In China and India, the demand came as a result of their strong economic growth. In the European Union's case, the demand came from citizen-investors concerned about the growing sovereign debt problem in a number of member states. The fiscally conservative Tea Party movement in the United States influenced the mid-term election, sending a Republican majority to the House of Representatives. The Federal Reserve announced the purchase of $600 billion in long-term Treasury bonds—a monetization of the national debt. The world's central banks, led by Russia and India, became net buyers of gold for the first time in decades. The International Monetary Fund sold over 400 tonnes in 2010, but it was absorbed readily with India purchasing 200 tonnes of the offer. In 2011, it is estimated that the world's central banks added 440 tonnes to their coffers—a level of interest that took the market by surprise. Commodity prices soared globally; an earthquake and tsunami devastated Japan; Osama bin Laden, the mastermind behind the 9/11 attack on the World Trade Center, was killed in a U.S. Navy SEALs operation in Pakistan. Debt problems intensified in Europe. France and the United States suffered downgrades of their vaunted AAA credit ratings. Gold hit a record price of $1895 in London in November 2011.

It is important for investors to understand that there is more to the gold market than the basic supply-and-demand tables that characterize other commodities. The story behind the tables—the history of gold—contributes substantially to its ebb and flow on the price charts. Beyond the fundamentals, gold is a political metal, and understanding its long history and its role in human affairs adds to an understanding of its place in the overall investment portfolio.

The annotated graphs above (Figures 21 through 26) tell the history of gold since 1971, as a good starting point to this understanding. The charts summarize the important key economic and political events that have accompanied gold's erratic upward climb.

P is for Post-1971 History of Gold—Study it well because the past might very well rhyme with the future.

Chapter 17

Q is for . . .
Quotable Notables on Gold

Thousands of words have been written over the centuries about gold—some flattering, some not. Although the world has changed considerably since gold was first used as money in ancient times, the varied human reactions to gold haven't changed at all over the centuries. Some have understood and valued gold. Others have seen it as an impediment to their political and economic designs. Some have seen it as a symbol of greed. Others have seen it as a symbol and instrument of freedom. Whatever the case, gold has indeed raised passions as well as a sense of practical security in the human soul, as noted in the following quotes supplied by the World Gold Council:

> There are about three hundred economists in the world who are against gold, and they think that gold is a barbarous relic—and they might be right. Unfortunately, there are three billion inhabitants of the world who believe in gold.
> —Janos Fekete (1918–2009)

> Regardless of the dollar price involved, one ounce of gold would purchase a quality man's suit at the conclusion of the Revolutionary War, the Civil War, the presidency of Franklin Roosevelt, and today.
> —Peter A. Bushre (1927–)

There can be no other criterion, no other standard, than gold. Yes, gold, which never changes, which can be shaped into ingots, bars, coins, which has no nationality and which is eternally and universally accepted as the unalterable fiduciary par excellence.

—Charles de Gaulle (1890–1970)

Water is best, but gold shines like fire blazing in the night, supreme of lordly wealth.

—Pindar (522–443 B.C.)

It is interesting to note that the average earnings of an English worker in 1900 came to half an ounce of gold a week and that in 1979, after two world wars, a world slump, and a world inflation, the British worker has average earnings of half an ounce of gold a week.

—William Rees-Mogg (1928–)

By common consent of the nations, gold and silver are the only true measure of value. They are the necessary regulators of trade. I have myself no more doubt that these metals were prepared by the Almighty for this very purpose, than I have that iron and coal were prepared for the purposes in which they are being used.

—Helen McCulloch (1808–1895)

Although gold and silver are not by nature money, money is by nature gold and silver.

—Karl Marx (1818–1883)

Like liberty, gold never stays where it is undervalued.

—J. S. Morill (1810–1898)

Gold is not necessary. I have no interest in gold. We'll build a solid state, without an ounce of gold behind it. Anyone who sells above the set prices, let him be marched off to a concentration camp. That's the bastion of money.
—Adolph Hitler (1889–1945)

The modern mind dislikes gold because it blurts out unpleasant truths.
—Joseph Schumpeter (1883–1950)

The tongue hath no force when gold speaketh.
—Guazzo

Even during the period when Rome lost much of her ancient prestige, an Indian traveler observed that trade all over the world was operated with the aid of Roman gold coins which were accepted and admired everywhere.
—Paul Einzig (1897–1973)

As good as gold...
—Charles Dickens (1812–1870)

You have to choose (as a voter) between trusting to the natural stability of gold and the natural stability and intelligence of the government. And with due respect to these gentlemen, I advise you, as long as the capitalist system lasts, to vote for gold.
—George Bernard Shaw (1856–1950)

It is extraordinary how many emotional storms one may weather in safety if one is ballasted with ever so little gold.
—William McFee (1881–1966)

Though wisdom cannot be gotten for gold, still less can it be gotten without it.
—Samuel Butler (1835–1902)

Gold opens all locks, no lock will hold against the power of gold.
—George Herbert (1593–1633)

Gold were as good as twenty orators.
—William Shakespeare (1564–1616)

Gold is a deep-persuading orator.
—Richard Barnfield (1574–1627)

The balance distinguisheth not between gold and lead.
—George Herbert (1593–1633)

Gold is a treasure, and he who possesses it does all he wishes to in this world, and succeeds in helping souls into paradise.
—Christopher Columbus (1451–1506)

In spite of all the romantic poets sing, this gold my dearest is a useful thing.
—Mary Leapor (1722–1746)

Gold is pale because it has so many thieves plotting against it.
—Diogenes (412–323 B.C.)

There can be no doubt that the international gold standard, as it evolved in the nineteenth century, provided the growing industrial world with the most efficient system of adjustments for balance of payments which it was ever to have, either by accident or by conscious planning.
—W.M. Scammell (1920–2007)

Not all that tempts your wandering eyes / And heedless hearts, is lawful prize / Nor all that glisten, gold.

—Thomas Gray (1716–1771)

Volumes could be filled with the many words, thoughts, and deeds surrounding gold. And, though times might change, it seems the attitudes of gold's defenders and detractors remain the same.

Q is for Quotable Notables on Gold—Coined wisdom from ages past.

Chapter 18

R is for . . .
Retirement Planning with Gold

As the ultimate long-term store of value, gold coins and bullion may very well be the ultimate retirement asset. Among the primary asset classes most often used in retirement planning—stocks, bonds, annuities, and savings accounts—gold stands out as the only one that does not rely on the performance of another individual or institution for value. This quality makes gold an ideal way to save for retirement at a time of economic uncertainty.

Precious metals retirement accounts, including Individual Retirement Accounts, were established under the Tax Reform Act of 1986. Precious metals retirement accounts are usually set up through gold firms that have a relationship with one or more trust companies. The client, in turn, opens a self-directed account with the trust company and funds it with contributions or a rollover. The final step is to purchase the precious metals you would like to include through your precious metals dealer. You then instruct the trust company to fund the purchase on your behalf. Once funded, the metals are deposited directly into your account. The trust company acts as intermediary in all buy-and-sell transactions. The metals are stored fully insured at a well-known depository facility. Many gold firms have specialists who can guide through the process of including gold in your retirement plan.

Under the Internal Revenue Code, there are specific precious metals products allowed. The purity standard for gold is .999 pure, or 99.9%; for silver, .995 or 99.5% pure; for platinum and palladium, .9995 or 99.95% pure. The one exception to the purity rule is the American Eagle gold coinage, which is .916 net fine or 91.6% pure. These standards narrow the range of choices. You can purchase bullion bars or bullion coins for your plan. Bars must be manufactured by exchange-approved refiners.

A list of allowable bullion coins follows:

- Approved gold bullion coins include the U.S. Eagle, the U.S. Buffalo, the Canadian Maple Leaf, the Australian Kangaroo, and the Austrian Philharmonic. These come in various sizes ranging from one troy ounce to one-tenth troy ounce.

- Approved silver bullion coins include the U.S. Eagle, the Canadian Maple Leaf, Austrian Philharmonic, and Mexican Libertad.

- Approved platinum coins include the U.S. Eagle, the Canadian Maple Leaf, the Australian Koala, and the Australian Platypus. There is only one approved palladium coin—the Canadian Maple Leaf. Proof American Eagles are also allowed but are not an advisable in a precious metals IRA due to vast premium disparities due to different interpretations of numismatic value. The best course of action is to stick with products from the above list that trade at lower premiums.

Transfers and Rollovers

Transferring a traditional or Roth IRA to a gold-backed IRA is relatively simple. Alternatively, the term "rollover" actually refers to the rolling over of assets from a 401(k) plan or some other qualified retirement plan to a self-directed IRA. In these cases, an employee must usually be separated from employment in order to establish a rollover.

Including precious metals in your retirement plan is a good idea, but make sure you approach the task under the guidance of a gold firm that has a good reputation and solid experience in this area. Generally speaking, the guidelines that apply to precious metals ownership outside your IRA also apply to owning the precious metals inside your IRA.

R is for Retirement Planning with gold—Make golden your golden years.

Chapter 19

S is for . . .

Storing Your Gold

Gold and love affairs are difficult to hide.
—Old proverb

You've done your homework. You've met with an experienced gold broker. You've purchased gold coins. Now what do you do with them?

Most investors take possession of their gold and make their own storage arrangements. The following are some of the most popular options.

Bank Safety Deposit Box

Gold can be stored in a safety deposit box at your bank. This is the option most gold investors exercise. The downside of safety deposit boxes is that items are not insured against theft, fire, flood, or similar disasters. Another potential problem is if the bank closes during a bank holiday, you may not be able to get to your gold when you most need it. The solution to this problem is to keep some at home and the bulk in the bank's safety deposit box. Although this particular storage solution has some drawbacks (as do all the other options), I believe this one to be the safest and most practical for the majority of gold owners.

Personal Safe

Another option is to store your gold at home or at the office in your own safe. Be careful here. I recommend a floor safe because it's easy to hide and difficult to crack. A freestanding safe will also do the job. However, insurance companies usually rate floor safes higher than freestanding safes. If you are thinking about storing gold at home, you might want to consult with a bonded safe company on the various options. You might also consider discussing the matter with your insurance agent before purchasing a safe. Your insurance company might offer coverage on your homeowner's policy. Some will cover gold, others won't.

Midnight Gardening

"Midnight gardening"—burying gold on your property—is another option. There are storage canisters available that do not corrode when buried. When considering midnight gardening, keep in mind the story of the man who purchased a respectable amount of gold and buried it in his backyard. Several years later he sold the house but forgot about his buried gold. He had to make a commando raid in his old backyard in the wee hours of the morning to recover it. There have also been cases of children and widows of the deceased being unable to find buried gold.

In my career as a gold broker, I have had some unusual calls about hidden gold. In one instance, a daughter called to say that she had reviewed several invoices for gold purchased by her now deceased father from my gold firm. Her mother was deceased as well, and before her father's death he had not told his daughter where he had hidden the gold. She hoped her father had disclosed the hiding place to me; unfortunately, he hadn't.

In another instance, a distraught wife, whose husband was not a client of the firm, called to ask if I had any general ideas where somebody might store gold. He had purchased a large amount of gold and hidden it. He had suffered a stroke that paralyzed him and left him unable to speak. He could not tell her where the gold was hidden.

Though fraught with peril, midnight gardening will always remain the chosen option for some gold owners.

Approach it with due diligence and care. Always leave instructions that can be easily found by your heirs for where you have hidden gold, or disclose your hiding place to loved ones in case of unforeseen incidents. Leaving a note in your safety deposit box is a common practice.

Depository Storage Accounts

If none of the options above suits you, the last option is to open an insured depository storage account. Most of the top gold firms can refer you to a reputable storage facility. The insured storage option is particularly helpful to silver owners who do not wish to deal with the bulk and weight problems it presents. There are two types of storage: Fungible and non-fungible. Fungible, or unallocated, storage means your gold is pooled with the gold of other depositors. There is no tagging or separation. Non-fungible, or allocated, storage means your gold is tagged and segregated. There is no pooling. Most gold owners prefer non-fungible storage because the specific coins or bars they purchased will be sent to them when delivery is requested. With fungible accounts, there are more-complicated procedures if you should request delivery, so they are less appealing to investors who know they will someday want their gold in hand.

One of the advantages of insured depository accounts is the ability to buy and sell over the phone without having to actually ship the metal. This allows the owner to trade his or her account easily and quickly. Some firms offer trading accounts that feature narrow buy/sell spreads and the ability to capture a price over the telephone. In most precious metals transactions, the metal must be received at the dealer's facility, or proof of shipment must be supplied, before a price can be set. Individuals who already have sufficient physical holdings in their possession and need a low-cost, reliable vehicle for trading in and out of the various precious metals for speculative purposes often establish depository accounts.

Arrangements can be made for delivery at some point along the way if the account holder so wishes.

S is for Storing Your Gold—Keep it safe; keep it for a rainy day.

Chapter 20

T is for . . .

Ten Memorable Vignettes on Gold and the Value of Money

Here is a collection of short readings on gold and the economy. In each case, these vignettes leave the reader with a thought or lesson worth filing for future reference and/or passing along as dinner table conversation. Enjoy!

Fighting Inflation in 1795 France

One of the remarkable points made by Andrew Dickson White in *Fiat Money in France* is that the French power structure was willing to embark on a money-printing scheme despite fully understanding the devastating inflationary experience at the hands of John Law several decades earlier. The French revolutionary government convinced itself that this time it would be different because France had become a Republic and shed the tyranny of the monarchy. Of course, events proved this rationalization wrong. The French "assignat inflation" devastated the French economy just as mercilessly as John Law's.

"The 'louis d'or' [gold coin]," says White, "stood in the market as a monitor, noting each day, with unerring fidelity, the decline in value of the 'assignat' a monitor not to be bribed, not to be scared. As well might the National Convention try to bribe or scare away the polarity of the mariner's compass. On August 1, 1795, this gold 'louis' of 25 francs was worth in paper, 920 francs; on September 1st, 1,200 francs; on November 1st, 2,600 francs; on December 1st, 3,050 francs. In February, 1796, it was worth 7,200 francs or one franc in gold was worth 288 francs in paper."

As White's example demonstrates, gold cannot be categorized as being in a bubble as long as the currency in which it is denominated is being systematically debased. It will continue to rise in value in rough proportion to the currency's loss of purchasing power until such time that faith in the currency is restored.

Yap Inflation One of the More Interesting in History

Monetarily speaking, everything progressed smoothly on the island of Yap where large stones weighing hundreds of pounds were transported around to serve as money. That is until something unforeseen happened to the value of the money. For centuries, the stones served in exchange because there wasn't much of this type of rock on Yap itself. The depreciation of the stone money began when an enterprising Western businessman realized he could produce stone money cheaply and in copious quantities on a neighboring island and transport it to Yap, where it could be used to procure goods in demand elsewhere. In other words, this oceanic cousin of John Law printed Yap stone money to buy his wares at what might be called a "favorable" discount. Little did the citizens of Yap know that they were deprived of their savings, and their money destroyed, by the process of monetary inflation.

Where is the United States in Alexander Tyler's Famous Progression?

Historian Alexander Tyler's once observed the following:

"A democracy cannot exist as a permanent form of government. It can only exist until the voters discover that they can vote themselves money from the public treasury. From that moment on the majority always votes for the candidates promising the most money from the public treasury, with the result that a democracy always collapses over loose fiscal policy followed by a dictatorship. The average age of the world's great civilizations has been two hundred years. These nations have progressed through the following sequence: from bondage to spiritual faith, from spiritual faith to great courage, from courage to liberty, from liberty to abundance, from abundance to selfishness, from selfishness to complacency, from complacency to apathy, from apathy to dependency, from dependency back to bondage."

Tyler made this famous observation with reference to ancient Athens, but few Americans would reflect on his progression without feeling a bit disconcerted. There is room for debate as to which rung on Tyler's continuum America occupies, but there is little doubt that it fulfills his most important criteria: Voters, as well as myriad special interest groups, have availed themselves to a large extent of the public treasury.

One Ounce of Gold = One Fine-Quality Man's Suit

The United States Geological Survey stated the following fact:

"The price of a fine suit of men's clothes can be used to show anyone who is not familiar with the price history of gold just how very cheap gold is today. With an ounce of gold, a man could buy a fine suit of clothes in the time of Shakespeare, in that of Beethoven and Jefferson, and in the depression of the 1930s. In fact, this statement was still true in the 1980s, but not in the late 1990s."

At this writing in early 2012 a call to a quality men's clothier in Denver's Cherry Creek district produced the following price list for a fine Italian-made man's suit:

- The best = $6000
- Mid-range but still high quality = $3500

In either instance the vest is not included. Gold is still clearly undervalued by this time-tested benchmark.

Anyone Can Inflate with a Little Effort

The *Financial Times* editorialist Martin Wolf once commented, "As Robert Mugabe has shown, anybody can run a printing press successfully." Or to put it another way, if you can push on a string in Zimbabwe, you can certainly accomplish the same in the United States with a little effort. Or to put it still another way, you can destroy the value of any paper currency if you try hard enough, as Robert Mugabe has done in Zimbabwe.

In 1923 Germany an Ounce of Gold Cost 63 Trillion Marks, Give or Take a Few Billion

Take into consideration the nightmare inflation that took hold in the period between the First and Second World Wars in Germany. Famed economist John Maynard Keynes summed it up nicely: "The inflationism of the currency systems of Europe has proceeded to extraordinary lengths. The various belligerent governments, unable, or too timid or too short-sighted to secure from loans or taxes the resources they required, have printed notes for the balance."

At the beginning of World War I (1914), an ounce of gold in Germany's Weimar Republic cost 86.8 marks. By November of 1923, the hyperinflationary blow-off drove the price of an ounce of gold to a staggering 63,016,800,000,000 (paper) marks. (Yes, that's 63 TRILLION marks!) Before you go to the calculator to decipher that return on an annualized basis, keep in mind that those who owned gold in Germany in 1922 did little more than simply hold onto their wealth by the end of 1923—far from a disappointing outcome given the circumstances.

America at the Tipping Point

Consider this from Hayman Advisors:

"Western democracies, communistic capitalists, and Japanese deflationists are concurrently engaging in what may be the largest global financial experiment in history. Everywhere you turn, governments are running enormous fiscal deficits financed by printing money. The greatest risk of these policies is that the quantitative easing will persist until the value of the currency equals the actual cost of printing the currency (which is just slightly above zero)."

"There have been 28 episodes of hyperinflation of national economies in the 20th century, with 20 occurring after 1980. Peter Bernholz (Professor Emeritus of Economics in the Center for Economics and Business (WWZ) at the University of Basel, Switzerland) has spent his career examining the intertwined worlds of politics and economics with special attention given to money. In his most recent book, *Monetary Regimes and Inflation: History, Economic and Political Relationships*, Bernholz analyzes the 12 largest episodes of hyperinflations—all of which were caused by financing huge public budget deficits through money creation. His conclusion: the tipping point for hyperinflation occurs *when the government's deficit exceed 40% of its expenditures.*" [Emphasis added.]

The on-budget U.S. deficit (not including borrowing from the Social Security fund) for 2009 was 51% of expenditures; for 2010, 47%; and for 2011, 44%.

Gold and Economic Freedom Redux

Ron Paul tells the story of his owning an original copy of *Gold and Economic Freedom*, Alan Greenspan's famous tome written as a young man. It begins with the oft-quoted and memorable line: "An almost hysterical antagonism toward the gold standard is one issue which unites statists of all persuasions." Congressman Paul remembers asking Greenspan to sign it. While doing so, Paul asked him if he still believed what he wrote in that essay some forty years before when he was a devotee of Ayn Rand. It is a strongly worded, no-holds-barred attack on fiat money and the central banks as an engine of the welfare state. It also endorses the gold standard as a deterrent to politicians' penchant for running deficits and printing money.

Greenspan—enigmatic as ever—responded that he "wouldn't change a single word." Several years later, in 2011, when a number of policy-makers publicly endorsed gold playing a role in a new monetary system, Greenspan, now retired as chairman of the Federal Reserve, stuck to his guns, speaking favorably once again about a return to the gold standard forty-five years after *Gold and Economic Freedom* was first published.

Humility on the Rubicon

Fed chairman Ben Bernanke, from a speech to the Council on Foreign Relations, as reported by Reuters in 2009:

> "Financial crises will continue to occur, as they have around the world for literally hundreds of years. Even with the sorts of actions I have outlined here today, it is unrealistic to hope that financial crises can be entirely eliminated, especially while maintaining a dynamic and innovative financial system. Nonetheless, these steps should help make crises less frequent and less virulent, and

so contribute to a better functioning national and global economy."

We have crossed a Rubicon of understanding when it comes to gold ownership and arrived in a new era with a new collective mind-set. Mr. Bernanke states it well and inadvertently makes a strong case for gold ownership. The certain knowledge that we live in an imperfect world prone to imperfect outcomes encourages one to put away a little of the yellow metal. Policy-makers did not talk like this one year ago. Chastened by events, common sense has suddenly made a comeback—a ray of light in a pitch-black room. While the policy-makers struggle to sort things out, gold owners retain the advantage of a good night's sleep—even during the worst of times—and that's a heady advantage.

How to Become the Richest Country in the World in One Easy Lesson

There may be something of a misunderstanding with respect to the increase in Chinese gold reserves. The bulk of that gold has come from purchases of their own domestic production, not open-market purchases. The impact on the price is therefore indirect. However, because China is the largest gold producer in the world, and it is retaining the bulk of its production for reserve diversification purposes, that impact is significant. Consider, for example, if South Africa had been able to retain the bulk of its production during the years it was the prime producer. It would today be one of the richest countries in the world.

T is for Ten Memorable Vignettes—Offer one or two as dinner table conversation with a golden moral.

Chapter 21

U is for . . .
Using Gold as Money

Since ancient times, gold has served humanity reliably as both a store of value and a medium of exchange. Today, using gold as money seems completely out of place in a world moving toward the elimination of currency and its replacement with credit and debit cards and even cyber-money. Yet the possibility of an economic crash has led many investors to put some gold away specifically for the purpose of buying essentials, if the worst were to happen.

In most instances (even a breakdown), gold owners would sell their gold for the currency in use at the time through the services of a gold exchange, and then use that currency at the store to buy whatever it is they wish to buy. However, some believe that in an economic breakdown with no reliable currency alternative available, citizens will resort to hand-to-hand barter transactions between individuals wherein gold would be used directly as a currency.

Small Gold Bullion Coins

The smaller gold bullion coins (one-half, one-quarter, and one-tenth ounce) best serve these purposes. Of that group, the one-quarter-ounce coin is the most useful. Most of the countries that mint gold—including the United States, Austria, and Canada—produce coins in the one-quarter-ounce size. These are large enough to pass easily as currency from buyer to seller. They can be stacked, stored, and accumulated without the fear of losing a coin or two in the process—something that cannot be said for the smaller one-tenth-ounce coin. The premium is slightly higher on the one-quarter-ounce coin (over the one-ounce coin), because the cost of making a coin is roughly the same no matter the size.

Those who foresee a potential for using gold as money and who are concerned with seizure and privacy matters might consider owning pre-1933 European gold coins as a medium of exchange. These items approximate one-fifth to one-quarter ounce of gold, and are priced similarly to their contemporary equivalents. When you purchase goods, there are no reporting requirements on these coins for you or the seller, and they provide an extra degree of safety with respect to a potential ban on ownership.

Using Silver Coins

In addition, you might want to consider a bag or two of silver coins—$1000 face value, pre-1965 U.S. silver coins. U.S. silver dollars are still recommended occasionally for this purpose, but the premium is relatively high. The greatest advantage of silver dollars is that they fall under the 1933 dateline with respect to a gold call-in. Silver rounds and one-ounce silver coins of various manufacture, including the U.S. and Canadian mints, are another alternative, although the premiums are relatively higher than what you would pay for bullion bars.

Having money to barter could be crucial during an economic breakdown. It makes sense to have some gold and silver put away for this purpose. This is not a complicated problem. This advice should suffice in the event of a breakdown.

U is for Using Gold as Money—Hope you never need to put this chapter to use.

Chapter 22

V is for . . .
Vital Statistics

This chapter is a compilation of vital statistics for all those who have questions about gold's physical and chemical characteristics, but don't know where to get the answers.

Gold is one of the densest of all the chemical elements. It is the most malleable metal. One ounce of gold can be drawn into a wire about thirty-five miles long. Gold is chemically related to copper and silver. It is highly resistant to chemical change and cannot be dissolved in common acids. Gold does dissolve, however, in aqua regia (a mixture of nitric and hydrochloric acids) and in cyanide.

Chemical symbol for gold: Au

Atomic number: 79

Atomic weight: 196.967

Specific gravity: 19.32

Tensile strength: 11.9

Melting point: 1,063 degrees F

Hardness (Brinell): 25

Occurrence of gold in the earth's crust: 0.005 parts per million

Estimated mine production: 165,000+ tonnes since gold was first discovered

First gold coin: Minted by Croesus of Lydia about 560 B.C.

Weights & Measures
1 troy ounce = 480 grains
1 troy ounce = 20 punts
3.75 troy ounces = 10 tolas (Indian Subcontinent)
6.02 troy ounces = 5 taels (China)
32.15 troy ounces = 1 kilogram
32,150 troy ounces = 1 metric ton (1,000 kilos)
1 troy ounce = 1.0971 ounce avoirdupois (U.S.)

Standard Investment Bar Sizes
400 troy ounces (12.5 kilos)
32.15 troy ounces (1 kilo)
100 troy ounces (3.11 kilos)
10 troy ounces
1 troy ounce

In addition, a wide variety of smaller bars by various manufacturers is not deliverable to any exchange, but trades among makers in smaller markets.

Troy weight is based on a pound of 12 ounces and an ounce of 480 grains. It is the universal measure by which gold is weighed and sold in all international markets.

Carat Gold Conversions
24-carat = 0.995 to 0.9999 pure (fine) gold
22-carat = 0.916 pure (fine) gold
18-carat = 0.750 pure (fine) gold
14-carat = 0.583 pure (fine) gold
10-carat = 0.4167 pure (fine) gold

Gold jewelry purity is always classified in carats (also *karats*). A carat is the traditional measure of purity contained in the alloy of gold used to make a piece of jewelry; the scale ranges from 1 to 24, with 24-carat representing pure gold.

Carat measure is seldom applied to bullion or bullion coin products.

The foregoing is not meant to be a complete compilation of gold's vital statistics, but merely an attempt to cover some of the more salient terms and characteristics encountered by gold investors on a regular basis.

V is for Vital Statistics—In case someone asks.

Chapter 23

W is for . . .
Wealth Insurance

The United States has become a nation of savers. Where once investors flocked to investment markets in the quest for wealth, they now flee them in order to preserve it. Saving is *in*. Speculation is *out*. After the loss of billions in stock market and real estate values, investors have returned to Old World notions about working hard, building businesses, practices, and careers; and investing prudently, as the real road to wealth and financial security.

The fanciful idea that one could simply day-trade, flip, or leverage his or her way to the leisure class has given way to the more conservative notion that wealth is built over time through the exercise of good judgment and strong doses of patience and hard work. The personal savings rate—the amount of income individuals set aside in low-risk instruments like savings accounts and money market funds—hovered in the 12% ranges in 1960s. By 2007, just prior to the financial meltdown, that figure had hit an all-time low of just over 2%. Immediately after the financial crisis of 2008, the savings rate began to rise, hitting an interim high of just over 7% in 2009. Since then it has hovered in the 4.5% to 5% range—quite a turnaround in the longer-term trend. Keep in mind, too, that this shift in sentiment occurred at a time when the yield on savings instruments was at all-time lows.

Though many, as Rudyard Kipling put it, will "wobble" their "bandaged finger" back to the flame, a good many others will strive to resist the temptation.

Savers today are confronted with a different, more dangerous set of economic circumstances from savers of the past. Polls show that many Americans have lost faith in their political and financial institutions. At the time of the John F. Kennedy administration in the 1960s, 80% of Americans believed that the federal government could be trusted "just about always or most of the time to do the right thing." By 2010, only 17% had that same faith—the lowest rating in modern history. Similarly, a CNN poll asked, "How much do you trust Wall Street bankers and brokers to do what is best for the economy?" One-half answered, "not at all." Sixty-five percent responded that they see Wall Street bankers and brokers as "greedy," "overpaid," and "dishonest."

I do not believe it would be a stretch of the truth to say that similar polling conducted in other countries around the world about their own political and financial leadership would produce similar results. Conversely, as mentioned in a previous chapter, a Gallup poll conducted in the summer of 2011 reported that Americans rated gold the best long-term investment "regardless of gender, age, income or party ID..." Americans, it would seem, are increasingly putting their faith in gold. Gold is not included in the national savings rate numbers, but perhaps it should be.

When you purchased this book, it was probably with the hope of finding answers to three simple questions:

- First, how do I go about adding gold to my portfolio?
- Second, is gold still the best way to protect my wealth even after its price run-up over the past several years?
- Third, are the conditions that created the bull market for gold in the 2000s likely to continue into the second decade of the twenty-first century?

This book offers concrete, utilitarian answers to the

first two questions. Any answer to the third question, however, remains a matter of opinion even though a growing list of economic thinkers have begun to reflect on the seeming stubbornness and longevity of the economic problem. "The pace and severity of financial crises have taken an ominous turn for the worse," says Stephen Roach, the chairman of Morgan Stanley Asia. "Over the past 30 years, a crisis has occurred, on average every three years. Yet now only about 18 months after the meltdown of 2008, Europe's sovereign debt crisis has hit with full force...Each crisis has its poster child—from Thailand, to dotcom to subprime. But they all have one thing in common—easy money. The 'Greenspan put'—the notion that central bankers would be quick and aggressive in backstopping financial market disruptions—was the short term anesthetic that repeatedly set the stage for the next crisis." His thinking takes us back to an earlier chapter in this book on the Great American Bailout of 2008–2010 and the aggressive response by both the U.S. federal government and its central bank.

It is worth repeating that, in 2011, the demand for gold coins and bullion globally rose by nearly 25%, according to the World Gold Council, and central bank demand rose nearly sixfold. Investment demand since the bull market began in 2003 is up 473%. There is an implicit warning in those statistics that should not be overlooked, and it has to do with the nature of owning any type of insurance, including the kind that is carried to protect investment portfolios. It is always less expensive and less psychologically stressful to buy before the event rather than after. Developments in the gold market in Greece at the height of its economic crisis are a case in point.

As it became apparent that there was not going to be an easy way out of its sovereign debt crisis, reports filtered into the gold market that the Greek people were buying substantial amounts of gold. In the first four months of 2010, according to one report, Greek citizens purchased over 50,000 British gold Sovereigns from their central bank, and it was rumored that another 100,000 British Sovereigns changed hands in the black market. At times, premiums ran 40% over melt, the result of ramped up demand. Now consider for a moment what might happen to gold coin demand during a *global* financial meltdown. It is a form of insurance that is in limited supply and subject directly to the laws of supply and demand. Timing is not an issue with gold. The essential question, if you agree with analysts who think like Mr. Roach, is whether or not you own it.

W is for Wealth Insurance—Buy it before you need it.

Chapter 24

X is for . . .

XYZ An Epilogue: The Once and Future Age of Economic Uncertainty

When the international monetary system was linked to gold, the latter managed the interdependence of the currency system, established an anchor for fixed exchange rates, and stabilized inflation. When the gold standard broke down, these valuable functions were no longer performed and the world moved into a regime of permanent inflation."

—Robert A. Mundell,
Nobel Laureate for Economics, 1999

Throughout this book, I have tried to offer the kind of practical advice I would provide any client who asked for it. I have tried to picture myself sitting with a potential gold buyer and answering the typical questions he or she would ask, if we both had the time to cover the various aspects of gold ownership in great detail. In parting, allow me to offer one more piece of practical advice and then I will send you on your way toward that initial (or next) gold purchase.

Had the United States and the rest of the industrialized world not embarked on a course in 1971 to remove gold from the monetary system, private ownership of gold would have been viewed as essentially redundant. The currency would have been as good as gold, and the need for the discussions, to which the bulk of this book addresses itself, would have been rendered unnecessary. In fact, this writer, who decided to become a gold broker

Figure 27. **Gold Standard versus Fiat Dollar Standard, (1900–2011)**

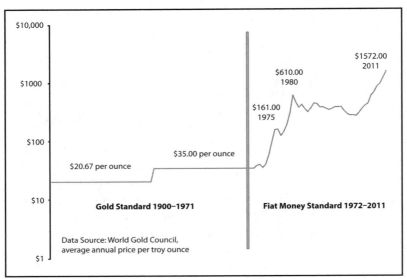

in 1971 when the dollar was first devalued formally by the Nixon administration, would have opted for an entirely different line of work.

As it is, the United States *did* fly from under gold's wing; its finances and the economy, as predicted, *did* take a turn for the worse; individuals in increasing numbers *did* take matters into their own hands by becoming private owners of gold coins and bullion; and I found myself an advocate for owning a metal that would soon become the financial system's lightning rod.

Over the course of four decades, I have watched from the catbird's seat gold's long evolution from "barbarous relic" to shunned pariah, then from ignored nuisance to respectable portfolio stalwart, and finally to reconsideration as a centerpiece in the world's financial system. It has been an interesting journey. If the world, as Robert Mundell suggests, has "moved into a regime of permanent inflation," over the past forty years, then gold has moved with it to take on a more a permanent and crucial role in the portfolio worldwide as a reliable store of value.

The Once and Future Age of Economic Uncertainty

The title to the best-selling book, *This Time Is Different—Eight Centuries of Financial Folly* (2009), by economists Carmen Reinhart and Kenneth Rogoff, is tongue-in-cheek. The theme of the book is that the crisis that began in 2008 is not significantly different from the myriad crises that preceded it, and contained within that sweeping conclusion is a lesson for investors far and wide.

Say Reinhart and Rogoff:

> "Of course financial crises are nothing new. They have been around since the development of money and financial markets. Many of the earliest crises were driven by currency debasements that occurred when the monarchy of a country reduced the gold and silver content of the coin of the realm to finance budget shortfalls often prompted by wars. Technological advances have long since eliminated a government's need to clip coins to fill a budget deficit. But financial crises have continued through the ages and they plague countries to this day."

The fact that much of the world is now immersed in a financial crisis is nothing new to anyone seriously considering the role of gold in his or her portfolio. What may be new, however, is that the circumstances that brought about the current crisis are not wholly different from those that created similar circumstances in centuries past, not to speak of the long list of crises since 1971. Those observations fold neatly into one of the main themes of this book, that is, the fiscal and monetary policies that caused the problems in 2008 have never really been addressed, thus paving the way for a similar crisis in the not-too-distant future.

In a later interview with the *Financial Times* (early 2012), Kenneth Rogoff reveals that "one of the reasons that Carmen Reinhart and I hit it off, is that we are both incredibly cynical about governments." Though I cannot vouch for the contents of Mr. Rogoff's investment portfolio, such cynicism, it has been my experience, more often than not beats a path to gold's door. Reinhart and Rogoff end the preface to the book with this prediction: "Unfortunately even before the ink is dry on this book, the answer will be clear enough. We hope that the weight of evidence in this book will give future policy makers and investors a bit more pause before next they declare, *"This time is different." It almost never is.*

True to form, by the end of 2011 the United States had lost its triple A credit rating, as had France, Greece, Italy, Austria, Belgium, and Portugal. What's worse, those credit ratings stand the chance of being cut further while the contagion effect threatens to dismantle ratings for countries that have thus far escaped the downgrades. Before the "ink is dry on *this* book," I have little doubt we will have moved to the next level of the international financial crisis. To be sure, concerns about the future of the U.S. and global economy have prompted a new age of economic uncertainty, though the remedy with respect to safeguarding private wealth is old indeed.

I would like to close this book with a thoughtful rationale for gold ownership from British parliamentarian Sir Peter Tapsell. Delivered before the House of Commons in 1999, Tapsell spoke these words in opposition to then Chancellor of the Exchequer Gordon Brown's plan to liquidate more than half of Britain's once-treasured gold reserve.

"The whole point about gold," he said, "and the quality that makes it so special and almost mystical in its appeal, is that it is universal, eternal and almost indestructible. The Minister will agree that it is also beautiful. The most enduring brand slogan of all time is, 'As good as gold...' The scientists can clone sheep, and may soon be able to clone humans, but they are still a long way from being able to clone gold, although they have been trying to do so for 10,000 years. The Chancellor (Gordon Brown) may think that he has discovered a new Labour version of the alchemist's stone, but his dollars, yen and euros will not always glitter in a storm and they will never be mistaken for gold."

These words are profound. They capture the essential nature of gold ownership. His reference to "dollars, yen and euros" had to do with the British treasury's proposal to convert the proceeds of the sale to "interest-bearing" instruments denominated in those currencies. Though Sir Tapsell was addressing gold's function with respect to the reserves of a nation-state, he could have just as easily been talking about gold's role for the private investor. Nation-states, in fact, look to derive the very same safeguards from gold that the private investor does.

In the end, the British government did sell over one-half of its gold—a policy that earned the description, Brown's Folly. Over the ensuing twelve years, gold went from $300 per ounce to nearly $1900 per ounce as the world economy moved through the first stages of a major financial breakdown. The "dollars, yen and euros" that the Bank of England received in place of the gold have only continued to erode in purchasing power while paying a negligible to nonexistent return. Most certainly they did not "glitter in a storm" nor were they "mistaken for gold," as Sir Peter Tapsell predicted.

Ultimately, and this is the final bit of practicality with which I will leave you, the case for gold ownership in the modern era rests on a single fundamental premise: In the absence of the gold standard, the value of our money and the stability of our economy—and thus the safety of our assets—rests solely in the hands of politicians and central bankers. Though they may exhibit the best of intentions, their policies might not always deliver the results intended. Under the circumstances, individuals would be well served by putting their personal finances on the gold standard through a prudent diversification into gold coins and bullion. This book was written as a means to that end. It emphasizes the notion that it is a matter of common sense to prepare for the worst and hope for the best. If, in the end, it opens the door to your becoming a gold owner, then it will have served its purpose well.

Appendix

Historic Gold Prices
London's Gold Bullion Market
Yearly Average Price

Year	Price	Year	Price	Year	Price	Year	Price
1900	18.96	1921	20.58	1942	33.85	1963	35.09
1901	18.98	1922	20.66	1943	33.85	1964	35.10
1902	18.97	1923	21.32	1944	33.85	1965	35.12
1903	18.95	1924	20.69	1945	34.71	1966	35.13
1904	18.96	1925	20.64	1946	34.71	1967	34.95
1905	18.92	1926	20.63	1947	34.71	1968	39.31
1906	18.90	1927	20.64	1948	34.71	1969	41.28
1907	18.94	1928	20.66	1949	31.69	1970	36.02
1908	18.95	1929	20.63	1950	34.72	1971	40.62
1909	18.96	1930	20.65	1951	34.72	1972	58.42
1910	18.92	1931	17.06	1952	34.60	1973	97.39
1911	18.92	1932	20.69	1953	34.84	1974	154.00
1912	18.93	1933	26.33	1954	35.04	1975	160.86
1913	18.92	1934	34.69	1955	35.03	1976	124.74
1914	18.99	1935	34.84	1956	34.99	1977	147.84
1915	18.99	1936	34.87	1957	34.95	1978	193.40
1916	18.99	1937	34.79	1958	35.10	1979	306.00
1917	18.99	1938	34.85	1959	35.10	1980	615.00
1918	18.99	1939	34.42	1960	35.27	1981	460.00
1919	19.95	1940	33.85	1961	35.25	1982	376.00
1920	20.68	1941	33.85	1962	35.23	1983	424.00

Year	Price	Year	Price	Year	Price	Year	Price
1984	361.00	1991	362.11	1998	294.09	2005	444.74
1985	317.00	1992	343.82	1999	278.57	2006	603.46
1986	368.00	1993	359.77	2000	279.11	2007	695.39
1987	447.00	1994	384.00	2001	271.04	2008	871.96
1988	437.00	1995	384.17	2002	309.68	2009	972.35
1989	381.44	1996	387.73	2003	363.32	2010	1224.53
1990	383.51	1997	331.29	2004	409.72	2011	1571.52

Source: World Gold Council

Bibliography

To distill over forty years of study in the fields of economics, economic philosophy, political science, history, and social theory—not to speak of probably hundreds of tracts and analyses on gold and its role in modern society—is a difficult undertaking. The following books, monographs, and articles contributed directly or indirectly to the underlying theme of this book and its statistical support. As such, they deserve special recognition.

Economic Research, Federal Reserve Bank of St. Louis, *FRED*, various, 2012.

Federal Reserve Bank of New York, *FAQs: MBS (Mortgage-Backed Securities) Purchase Program*, 2009.

Federal Reserve Board Statistical Release, *Factors Affecting Reserve Balances of Depository Institutions*, 2012.

Gold Avenue. *Gold Encyclopedia & Diary*. London: 2004.

Gold Fields Mineral Services. *2011 Annual Gold Survey*. London: 2011.

Goodman, Avery, Midas Letter, *Gold at $210,000?*, 2011.

Green, Timothy. *The Gold Companion*. City: Rosendale Press, 1991.

Green, Timothy. *The New World of Gold*. New York: Walker and Company, 1984.

Greenspan, Alan. *Gold and Economic Freedom*. New York: 1967.

Grun, Bernard. *The Timetables of History: A Horizontal Linkage of People and Events.* New York: Simon and Schuster, 1991

Hathaway, John. *The Folly of Hedging.* City: Tocqueville Asset Management, LP, 2000.

Hatton, Tim. *The New Fiduciary Standard: The 27 Prudent Practices for Financial Advisers, Trustees and Sponsors,* Bloomberg Press, 2005.

Index Mundi, *Country Profiles,* 2012.

Jastrum, Roy. *The Golden Constant.* New York: John Wiley & Sons, 1977.

Jenkins, G.K. *Ancient Greek Coins.* New York: G.P. Putnam & Sons, 1972.

Kindleberger, Charles. *Manias, Panics and Crashes: A History of Financial Crises.* New York: John Wiley & Sons, 1978.

McGeveran, William A., Jr. (Editor). *The World Almanac and Book of Facts 2004.* New York: World Almanac Books, 2004.

Mineweb.com, Gold Analysis, various, 2011, 2012.

National Data Book. Washington, D.C.: U.S. Government Printing Office, 1995–2011.

Office Of Management and Budget, Historical Tables, 2012.

Rankin, Robert. *The Impact of Hedge Funds on Financial Markets: Lessons from the Experience of Australia.* City: Reserve Bank of Australia, 1999.

Reinhart, Carmen M. and Kenneth Rogoff. *This Time is Different: Eight Centuries of Financial Folly.* Princeton University Press, 2009.

Sack, Brian P., New York Federal Reserve, *The Fed's Expanded Balance Sheet,* 2009.

Scientific Market Analysis. *The Nightmare German Inflation.* Princeton, New Jersey: 1971.

Silver Institute, Supply-and-Demand Tables, 2011.

Teeple, John P. *Timelines of World History.* London: DK

Publishing, 2002.

Thornton, Daniel L., Vice-President-Economic Adviser, Federal Reserve Bank of St. Louis, *Monetizing the Debt*, 2010.

U.S. Department of Commerce. Economics and Statistics Administration. *The Statistical Abstract of the United States.*

U.S. Department of the Interior, U.S. Geological Survey, *Mineral Commodity Summaries*, 2011.

U.S. Department of the Treasury. *Treasury Bulletin.* Washington, D.C.; U.S. Government Printing Office, 1996–2011.

U.S. Department of the Treasury, Bureau of the Public Debt. *The Debt to the Penny.* Washington, D.C.: U.S. Government Printing Office, 2011.

U.S. Department of the Treasury, *Treasury International Capital Report (TIC)*, 2012.

Virtual Metals, *The Yellow Book*, 2011.

White, Andrew Dickson, *Fiat Money Inflation in France*, 1914.

World Gold Council. *Gold Demand Trends*, A Quarterly Publication. New York and London: 1996–2011.

World Gold Council. *The Gold Borrowing Market: A Decade of Growth.* Prepared by Ian Cox. Geneva, 1996.

World Gold Council. *The Management of Reserve Assets: Opportunities and Risks in a Multi-Currency System.* Prepared by Dr. H.J. Witteveen. Geneva: 1993.

World Gold Council. *America's Deficit, the Dollar & Gold.* Prepared by Tim Congdon. London: 2002.

Index

British Sovereign, 81, 83, 107, 164
Brown, G., 168–169
Brown's Folly, 169
Buffet, Warren, 4
bullion banks, 54
bullion coins *see* gold bullion coins
bull market, 52, 57, 123, 127
Bureau of Labor Statistics (BLS), 9
Bush, G. H. W., 124
Bushre, P. A., 137
Butler, S., 140

C

Cambior Mines, 126
Canadian Maple Leaf, 20, 23, 28, 143
carat (karat), 23, 159–160
Carter, J., 123
Central America, 15
Central Bank Agreement on Gold (CBGA), 56, 58–61, 63
central banks, 54–58
China, 11, 127, 135, 155
Christianity, 46
Christmas Surprise, 12
Churchill, W., 77
Civil War, 15, 137
client-oriented gold firms, 33–34
Clinton, B., 125
Clinton administration, 125
CNN, 162
Cold War, 125
Columbus, Christopher, 140
COMEX, 23–24, 99–101
commemorative coins, 93
Commodities Futures Trading Commission, 35, 119

commodity, gold as, 105–106
confiscation, 84
consumer price index, 6
Continental Dollar collapse, 15
core problem, 4
Council on Foreign Relations, 47, 154
counterfeiting, 24–25
credit cards, 156
creditor nation, 5
Croesus, Lydia, 26
currency
  fiat, 70
  gold as, 92, 156–157
  printing, option for, 69–71
  reserve, 11, 56, 67–68
  silver as, 157
  value of, 149–155
Curry, M., 49
customer-oriented gold firms, 33–34
cyber-money, 156

D

Damocles, 60
debit cards, 156
de Boton, A., 46–47
debt monetization, 70–71, 76–77, 86
debtor nation, 5
deflation, 70–71, 86–88, 92
deflationary abyss, 86
de Gaulle, C., 68, 138
de Lille, A., 20
Denver Gold Group, 59
depository storage accounts, 25, 147–148
d'Estaing, V. G., 68
Deutsche Bank, 54, 100
Dickens, C., 139

178

Index

global financial crisis/melt
down, 43–45, 111, 127–136,
161, 164
global inflation, 77
GLOBEX, 24, 101
gold *see also* specific topics on;
specific types of
buying, 39, 56–58
demand for, 55, 61–63, 135,
163
diversification of, 40–42
forms of, 20
fundamentals of, 63–64
history of, 121–136
importance of, 3
interest of, 18, 104–105
investment in, 15–17, 107–
109
lending, 54–56
measuring, 159
myths about, 104–109
need for, 15–19
ownership of, 85, 89–93,
115–120, 122
price of, 49–50, 107, 171–172
profiting from, 91
realities about, 104–109
seizure of, 78, 83, 90, 157
stocks vs., 105
storing, 145–148
supply of, 50–51, 51–54, 55
uses of, 3
value of, 1, 20, 108, 113–114,
149–155
vignettes on, 149–155
weight of, 159
Gold and Economic Freedom
(Greenspan), 154
gold-backed Individual
Retirement Accounts, 143

gold bars, 20, *see also* specific
types of
gold bullion bars, 2, 21, 24–25,
159
gold bullion coins, 20–30 *see
also* specific types of
availability of, 24
as currency, small, 156–157
demand for, 25–26, 163
denominations of, 21–22
locked-in-price of, 24
popular, 21–22
pricing of, 23–24
safe-haven status of, criteria
for, 31
trading, 22
gold bullion leaves, 2
gold coins, 20 *see also* specific
types of
gold exchange traded funds,
117–118
gold firms, 31–37
client-oriented vs. customer-
oriented, 33–34
credentials of, 35–36
expertise of, 34–35
historical establishment of,
32–33
instincts, trusting, 37
objectives, focus on, 37
pricing, comparisons of, 36
referrals to, 36
sales tactics used by,
aggressive, 34
selecting, 32
smart, 33
transactions, details about,
36–37
Goldilocks economy, 47–48
gold investors, types of, 89

Reuters, 154
Revolutionary War, 15, 137
Roach, S., 163–164
Rogoff, K., 167–168
rollover, 143–144
Roman aureus, 70
Roman Stoic philosophy, 46
Roosevelt, F. D., 78, 84–85,
    100, 121, 137
Roth Individual Retirement
    Accounts, 143
Rothschild Group, 54
Rubicon, 154–155
Ruskin, J., 43
Russia, 135

S

Sachsen Landesbank, 128
safe-haven investors, 31, 90–91
St. Louis Federal Reserve, 74–75
sales tactics, aggressive, 34
Saud, I., 107
Scammell, W. M., 140
Schels, S., 49
Schumpeter, J., 139
Scotia Mocatta, 54, 100
Securities and Exchange
    Commission, 35
self-directed Individual
    Retirement Accounts, 143
self-goals, 92–93
self-needs, 92–93
September 11, 2001 terrorist
    attacks, 127
Shadow Government Statistics,
    9
Shakespeare, W., 4, 140
Shaw, G. B., 139
Sigfusson, S., 69
silver, 94–97
    as currency, 157

as inflation hedge, 91
investment portfolio, role in,
    95
"Oh-Oh" decade, value of,
    113–114
price of, 95–96
supply-and-demand for,
    fundamentals of, 96–97
uses of, 97
silver bullion coins, 143
Silver Institute, 97
S&L crisis, 124, 124–125
Social Security, 5, 153
Societe General, 54, 100
South African Krugerrand, 20,
    22, 22–23, 30
South America, 15
Southeast Asia coin kit, 19
sovereign debt crisis/problems,
    15, 111, 128
Soviet Union, collapse of, 15,
    124
S&P (Standard and Poor),
    11–12
Spain, 128
SPDR Gold Trust, 117–118
speculative investors, 91
stagflation, 87–88
Steele, J., 56–57
stern labor, 43
stewardship, 44
stock market crash, 111, 116
stocks, 105, 111–112
Strauss, W., 110
supply-and-demand, 51, 56,
    96–97
Swiss franc, 8–9, 80, 83
Swiss national reserve, 126

T

Tapsell, P., 168–169

About the Author

Michael J. Kosares is the founder and president of USAGOLD, one of the oldest and most prestigious gold firms serving private gold investors. His book, *The ABCs of Gold Investing*, now in its third edition, is considered one of the top introductory manuals on gold ownership. He has been widely interviewed for his views on gold and the economy. He is also the author of numerous articles, essays, and booklets published regularly in a wide assortment of Internet websites and magazines. He also comments frequently on the state of the gold market and the economy at his USAGOLD website, www.usagold.com, and via randomly issued special reports on gold and the economy. Kosares may be reached by contacting USAGOLD, P.O. Box 460009, Denver, CO 80246. 1-(800) 869-5115.